Smriti Daniel

ROBOT Responders

Rescue Missions to Space Adventures

NATIONAL LIBRARY OF AUSTRALIA

A catalogue record for this book is available from the National Library of Australia

ISBN: 9781486318421 (pbk)
ISBN: 9781486318438 (epdf)
ISBN: 9781486318445 (epub)

Published by:
CSIRO Publishing
36 Gardiner Road, Clayton VIC 3168
Private Bag 10, Clayton South VIC 3169
Australia

Telephone: [+613] 9545 8555
Email: csiropublishing@csiro.au
Website: www.publishing.csiro.au
Sign up to our email alerts: publishing.csiro.au/earlyalert

Edited by Dr Kath Kovac
Cover, text design and layout by Cathy Larsen Design
Printed in China by Toppan Leefung Printing Limited

CSIRO acknowledges the Traditional Owners of the lands that we live and work on across Australia and pays its respect to Elders past and present. CSIRO recognises that Aboriginal and Torres Strait Islander peoples have made and will continue to make extraordinary contributions to all aspects of Australian life including culture, economy and science. The use of Western science in this publication should not be interpreted as diminishing the knowledge of plants, animals and environment from Indigenous ecological knowledge systems.

Note for teachers: Teacher notes are available at:
https://www.publishing.csiro.au/book/8165/#forteachers

Nov25_01

Contents

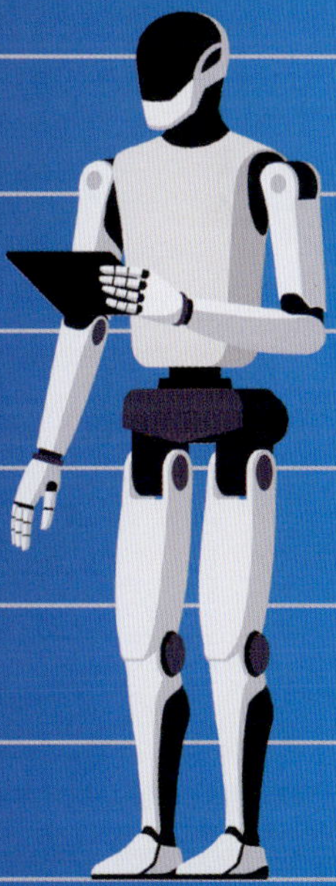

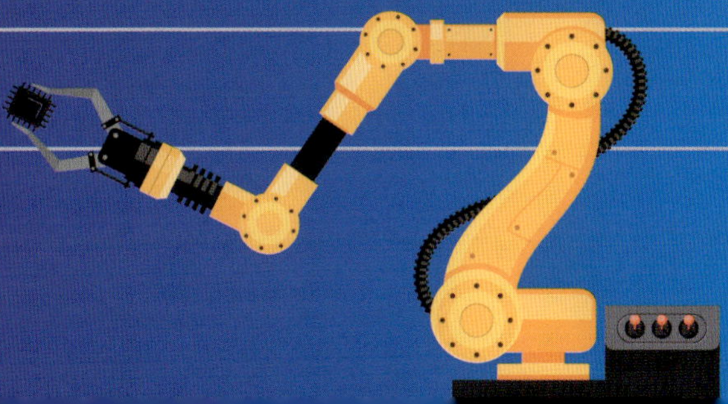

Preface

The first time I wrote down the word 'robot', I was 10 years old. It was in a shaky, messy hand. I hadn't yet learned how to write properly in cursive. So, my father made me practise every afternoon. The text I had to copy: pages from Isaac Asimov's book *Robots and Empire*.

I don't think my handwriting improved a great deal. That's because when my father got busy in the next room, I'd stop writing and simply keep reading.

I'll be honest. At the time, much of the book went right over my head. Still, I was fascinated! I read lots of Asimov's books after that. Even today, I still remember the three 'laws' that applied to the robots in his books:

1. A robot may not injure a human being or, through inaction, allow a human being to come to harm.
2. A robot must obey orders given by human beings, except where such orders would conflict with the First Law.
3. A robot must protect its own existence as long as such protection does not conflict with the First or Second Law.

I still love reading. And I've always suspected that writing was the only thing I was any good at. It led me to a career in journalism.

As a journalist, I visited NASA's Goddard Space Flight Centre in Maryland, outside Washington DC. It's where I had my first real close-up view of what robots in space could look like. I saw a replica of the Cassini–Huygens spacecraft. Its counterpart was in orbit around the alien moons of Jupiter! I also saw the great 6.5-metre wide mirrors of the new James Webb Space Telescope as it was being built. The 'Webb' was designed like a giant origami robot. It could be folded up so its massive mirrors would fit into a rocket. Once it got to outer space, it would unfold like a Transformer.

Neither of these space robots looked like the humanoid versions Asimov had imagined. But when I thought of everything they would see as they travelled to distant moons and planets, I was filled with awe.

Webb is now orbiting the Sun, 1.5 million kilometres away from Earth. It can see so far that it is effectively looking back in time to show us the first galaxies being born! I'll always consider seeing the Webb up close as a highlight of my career.

I now work at CSIRO, Australia's national science agency. Here, I get to interact with amazing scientists who bring incredible new technologies to life every day. They've even loaded new equipment onto a rocket and sent that to the International Space Station!

But robots aren't just out in space. They're all around us: helping fight fires, discover new species and explore the deep ocean. They work in our factories and hospitals. When I visited the National Gallery of Victoria in 2024, I even found robot dogs drawing pictures on the wall!

We can learn so much cool stuff about robots, and they have so much to teach us! We're also going to have to figure out how we live, work and play with them.

I'm so glad you're on this journey of discovery with me. Ready to dive in?

Smriti Daniel has always loved reading, writing and robots! (Image courtesy Alex Kwong, courtesy ActNow Theatre)

What to expect from this book

In this book, we're going to explore the world of robotics.

It's a fast-moving field that combines subjects such as engineering, computer science and maths to create innovative machines that can help us. I'm excited to share with you what I've learned and discovered about robots – from their earliest history to recent advancements. We'll even meet a few exceptional robots and the people who've built them.

We'll start by taking a journey through the history of robotics. You'll meet ancient mechanical figures, learn about the first computers, and discover how advances in technology have made today's robots possible.

Then we'll ask: what exactly is a robot? Essentially, a robot is a machine designed to perform tasks. Sometimes, these tasks are too dangerous or repetitive for humans, which is where robots can be really useful. Along the way, we'll explore how robots think, communicate and even how they 'see' and 'feel' the world around them.

As we dive deeper, you'll learn about roboticists – the scientists and engineers who create robots. They use their knowledge to design and build robots for all sorts of purposes, from exploring distant planets to helping doctors perform surgery.

Then, we'll compare humans and robots. You'll see that bots can learn and act in ways that might surprise you.

One of the most exciting areas we'll explore is biomimicry – how people design robots based on animals and nature. This approach has led to robots that can fly like birds, swim like fish and even climb like geckos.

Robots work in many different environments. We'll look at real-world examples of how robots move. How do they navigate on land, in water, in the air and even in space? You'll learn how they overcome the challenges they face in each of these places.

An important part of our exploration will be the ethical questions that arise with robotics. We'll discuss issues such as privacy, jobs and how robots should be treated. These are complex topics, but it's important to think about them as we rely more on robots.

Finally, we'll imagine the future of robotics. What new types of robots might we see? How will they change the way we live and work? The possibilities are as limitless as our imagination.

I wrote this book because I believe understanding robotics is not just about knowing how machines work. It also involves thinking critically about the role technology plays in our lives. Thinking ahead allows us to create solutions that are good for all of us.

I hope this journey inspires you to learn more – and maybe even become a roboticist yourself one day! Let's get started on this exciting adventure together.

01 A short history of robots

You and I live in an exciting moment in time, when huge scientific advances have allowed robotics to flourish. But before we look ahead and explore the robots of today and tomorrow, we need to understand that people have been dreaming and telling stories about – and even building – machines that could move and work like humans for a long time.

Each era, from the mythological automatons of ancient cultures to the sophisticated designs of the period known as the Renaissance, has seen its vision of robotics influenced by its unique understanding of the world.

Did you know?

The word robot comes from a Czech word, *robota*, which means forced labour or work.

The guardian of Crete

Around 2,700 years ago, Greek poets such as Hesiod and Homer imagined artificial beings. Within their verses, you'll meet creations so marvellous they blur the lines between gods, humans and machines.

Take the legendary Talos.

Hesiod described Talos as a sentinel – a watchman made entirely from bronze who towered high above ordinary people. Hephaestus was the god of invention and master of the forge. He crafted Talos to take on the monumental task of safeguarding Crete. The bronze watchman circled Crete three times a day and hurled boulders at any enemy ships he spotted.

Talos wasn't Hephaestus' only creation. The great blacksmith also made women out of gold. Famously, he gave these golden women the knowledge of the gods – strength, understanding and speech.

These early tales aren't just myths. They reflect the human desire to understand and recreate life itself. By exploring how ancient people imagined these mechanisms, we can see the roots of our modern fascination with robotic technology.

Winged 'ΤΑΛΩΝ' armed with a stone. Reverse side of silver didrachma from Phaistos, Crete (c. 300/280–270 BC). (Image courtesy Cabinet des Médailles, Paris)

Did you know?

Legends tell of mechanical beings that were set to guard the relics of the Buddha – the *bhuta vahana yanta*, which means spirit-movement machines in the Pali language of India. The stories say the mythical warriors, supposedly built by King Ajatasatru around 2,400 years ago, could whirl like the wind and slash intruders with swords.

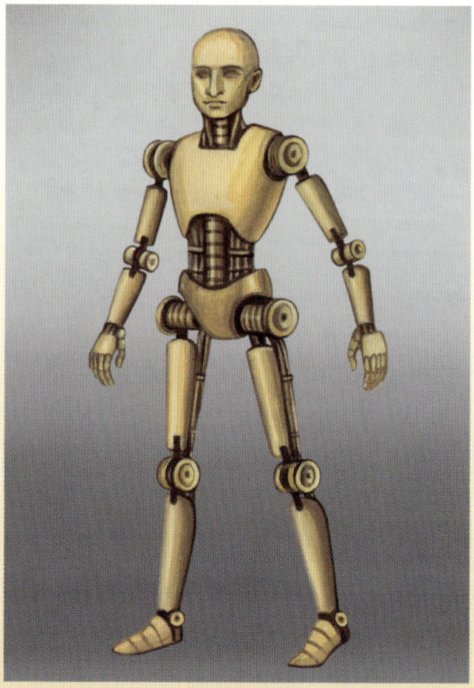

Beneath its exterior, a robot can have many moving parts, including gears and joints that help it move.

Talos, a giant watchman from Greek mythology, was said to be made entirely of bronze.

da Vinci's knight in shining armour

Did you know that Leonardo da Vinci – the famous artist who painted the Mona Lisa – was also into robots?

Leonardo was inspired by the human body and how it worked. And his design was quite extraordinary. He envisioned a mechanical knight in shining armour that could move its arms, turn its head and even lift its visor. It would do all this thanks to a clever system of gears and pulleys.

Around 1495, while working for the Duke of Milan, Leonardo might have even built his metal knight! Five hundred years later, NASA scientist Mark Rosheim was inspired by Leonardo's old designs.

As a child, Mark first heard of Leonardo from a book that his family babysitter was reading. As a teenager he read more books and even watched a television series about the Italian inventor.

'When I got to university, I would go to the library and look at Leonardo's books, and books about him,' Mark remembers. 'I was surprised to discover that Leonardo had designed robots. I stumbled upon a reference to Leonardo's last robots.'

Mark would go on to try and recreate some of those designs. One was a robotic cart, and the other was the knight.

In 2002, Mark was invited by the British Broadcasting Corporation to build a prototype. He succeeded in recreating Leonardo da Vinci's design. His model was able to walk and wave. It's like Leonardo's brilliant ideas jumped right out of history into our modern world!

Mark says the key to his success was persistence.

'I think it's all about determination. Some designs I've worked on for 20 years. I don't give up – I just keep moving forward.'

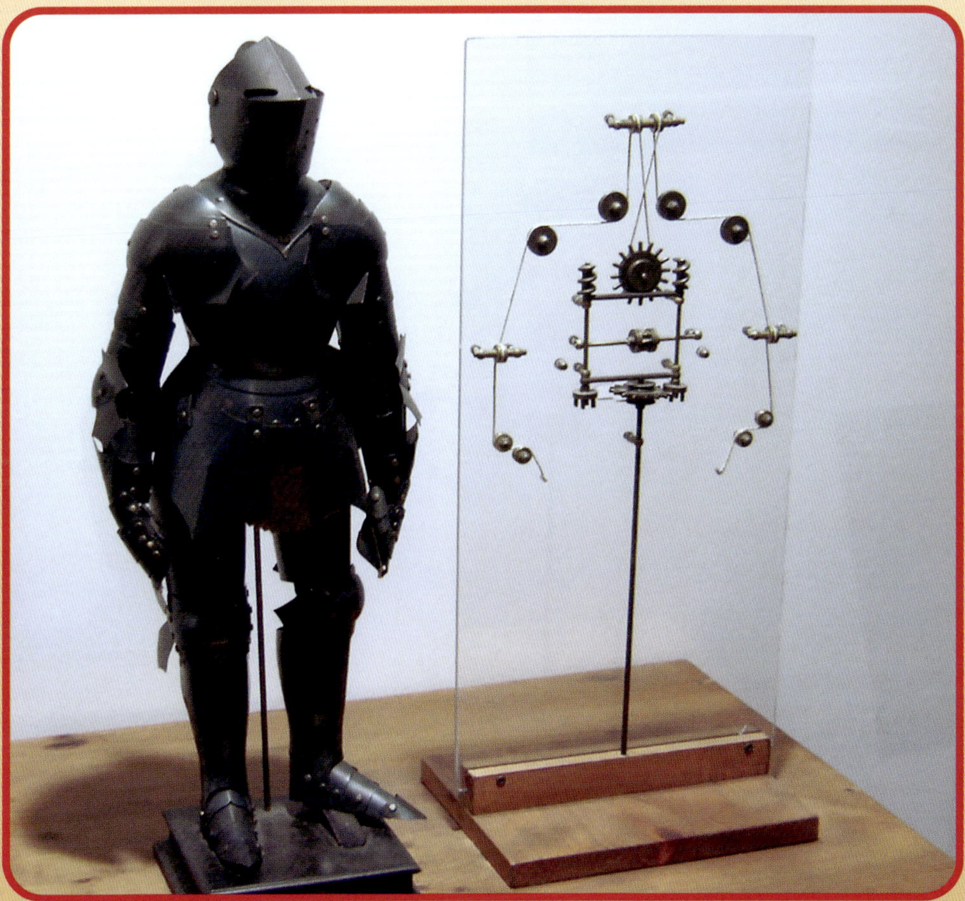

Model of a robot based on drawings by Leonardo da Vinci. (Image courtesy Erik Möller. Leonardo da Vinci. Mensch – Erfinder – Genie exhibit, Berlin 2005)

Illustration of a George III automaton elephant clock by Hubert Martinet, London, date circa 1770. It moves its trunk, ears and tail.

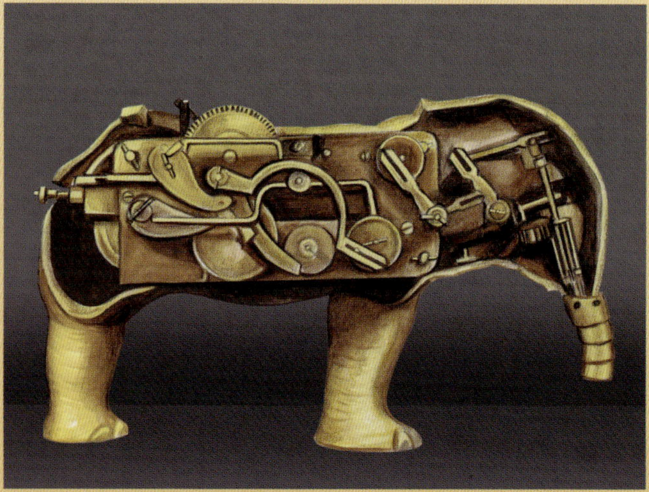

The inner workings of the automaton elephant clock.

Putting the art in automata

Before robots were automata (or-TOM-ah-ta) – the plural of automaton (or-TOM-ah-ton). These models relied on the ingenuity of human beings to create fantastical works of art that sparked amazement in everyone who beheld them.

From ancient Greece to 18th-century Europe, people have been fascinated by these incredible machines. Automata had intricate gears and levers and were powered by water, gravity or steam. They were a promise of what the future held.

As we delve into the history of automata, it's important to recognise the artists and thinkers, such as Leonardo da Vinci, who envisioned machines that mimicked human and animal movements. Their work laid the groundwork for inventors such as Pierre Jaquet-Droz.

Ethical questions: Robots at work

New technology, such as robots, often changes the types of jobs available for humans. We've seen this many times throughout history. For example, when cars became common, many jobs related to horse-drawn carriages disappeared. However, new jobs in car manufacturing and maintenance were created.

Change on this scale can be scary for those living through it. But it also opens up possibilities for exciting new careers and innovations that we might not have imagined yet. As we adjust to these changes, it's important to think creatively about how we can use technology to improve our world. This includes supporting those it affects the most!

What kinds of jobs do you think might disappear because of robots? And what new jobs do you think might be created in the future because of these technologies?

Did you know?

Automata are models of people or animals that appear to be moving independently, but are actually animated by a hidden clockwork mechanism.

Illustration of the Automate Therapaenis (automatic maid). This doll was described over 2,200 years ago, and could transfer liquids from two pots inside its body to a jug held in her hands.

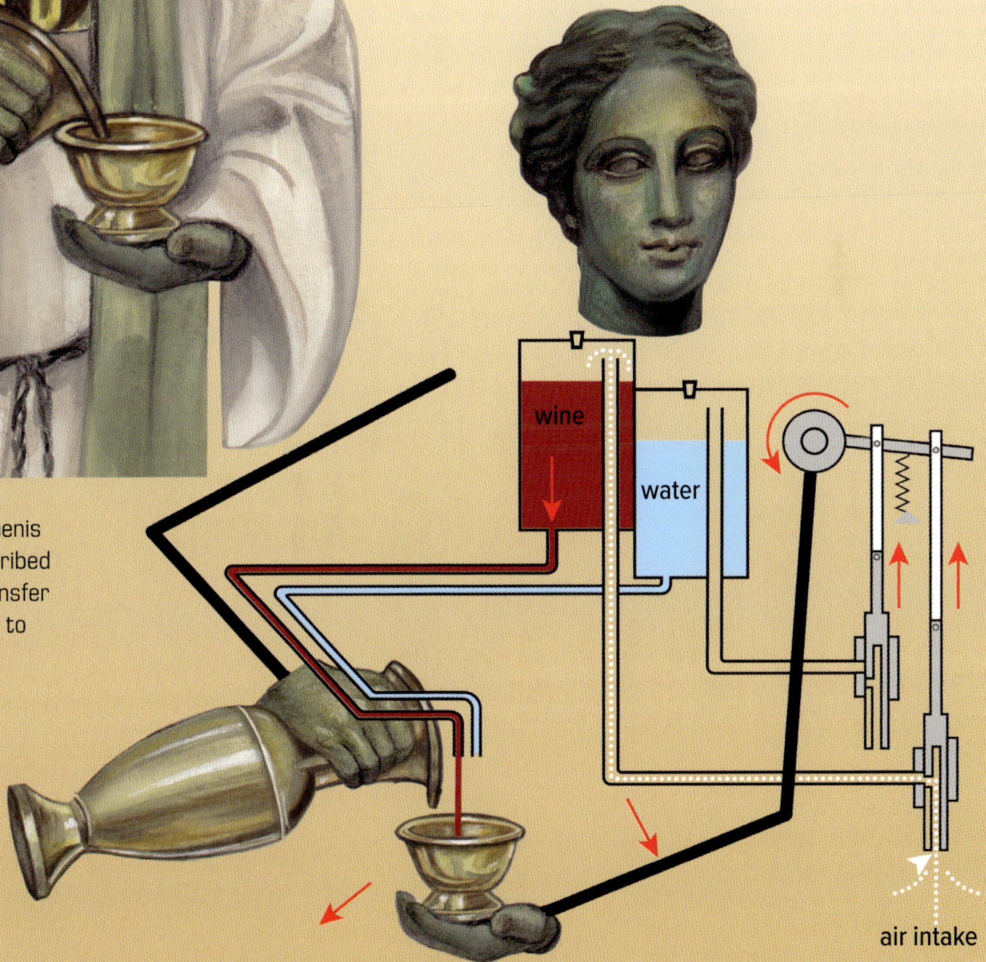

The Writer, The Draughtsman and The Musician

Pierre lived in the 1700s, and he was something of a genius. We credit him with some of the most exciting and clever examples of automata.

The Writer is one of his most famous creations. This wasn't just any toy. It had around 6,000 moving parts inside! The Writer could write custom text of up to 40 characters using a goose feather quill pen. It even knew how to dip the pen in ink and shake off the excess. Its eyes followed the text while writing, and its head moved when it refilled the ink.

Pierre also created a young artist called The Draughtsman. This automaton could draw four different images. It used a system of rotating or sliding pieces that were mechanically linked together. It even had a trick up its sleeve – it would blow on the pencil to clear any dust.

Last came The Musician. It played music on a custom-built organ. And it wasn't pre-recorded – it actually pressed the keys with its fingers! The Musician was so lifelike that it even 'breathed' and followed the movement of its hands with its head and eyes. When its performance was done, it took a bow.

Today, you'll find these amazing automata at the Musée d'Art et d'Histoire (Museum of Art and History) in Neuchâtel, Switzerland. And the best news? They still work.

Thanks to creators such as Pierre, we've learned how mechanics and art can come together to create something extraordinary – inspiring modern robotics.

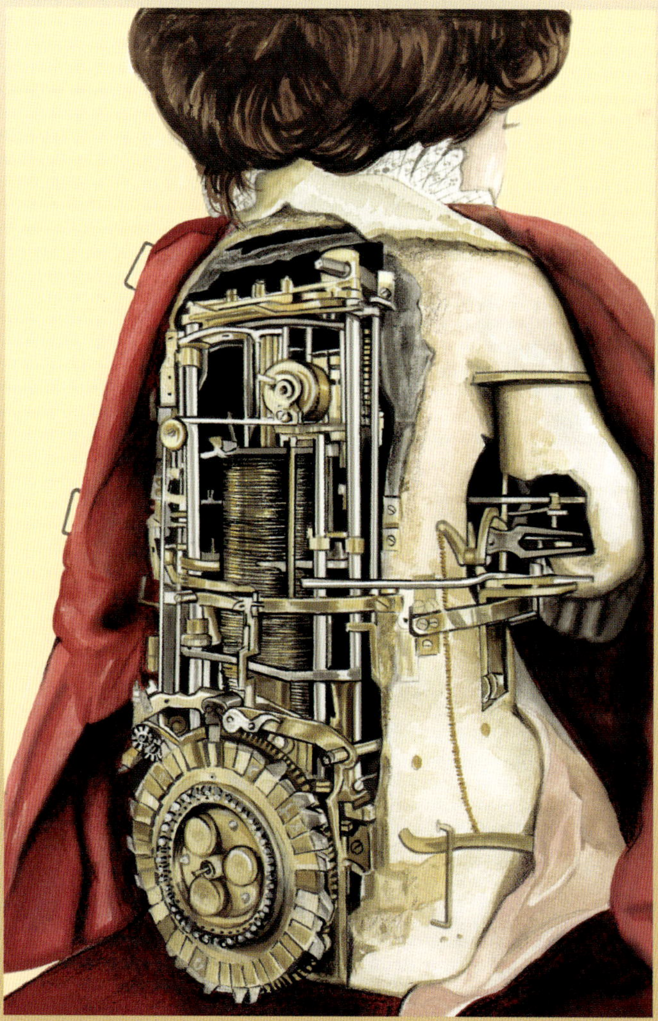

Historic Jaquet-Droz automata on display (top), with illustration of inner workings below. (Top image courtesy Rama, Wikimedia Commons, CC BY-SA 2.0 fr)

02 The digital revolution

While the automata of the past were marvels of mechanical art, today's robots blend these age-old dreams with new capabilities. A lot of this is possible thanks to huge advancements in materials and computing. It reflects the continuing quest to not just mimic life, but to improve it.

Unimate in the spotlight

Fast forward a few hundred years from the first automata, and the blueprint for robots as we recognise them today began to emerge.

A pivotal moment in 1961 saw the introduction of Unimate, often celebrated as the first industrial robot. Unimate was installed in a car factory in New Jersey, where it handled hot metal parts and did welding. These tasks had traditionally been quite risky for people and often led to injuries. It's why this robot was hailed as a game-changer in factories.

Unimate was pretty smart for its time. It had hydraulic lines running inside it, which helped it move its arm precisely. The end of its arm was pretty cool too – it could rotate and hold tools, somewhat like a hand.

Programming Unimate was a big task. Engineers used switches and timers to tell it exactly what to do. It didn't have the touch screens or buttons we might see on robots today. It communicated with other machines using simple electrical signals. This was way before Wi-Fi or Bluetooth, so it was pretty groundbreaking at the time.

Unimate was the start of a whole new era in robotics, making factories safer and more efficient.

The 3,500 pound (1,500 kilogram) industrial robot, Unimate, pouring coffee for a woman at Biltmore Hotel in Los Angeles, California, 1967. (Image courtesy Los Angeles Times Photographic Archive, UCLA Library Special Collections)

The evolution of robots

It could be said that the evolution of robots in the 20th century hinges on two breakthroughs: advances in computing and the development of new materials. Without these, our modern robots might have remained in the realm of science fiction.

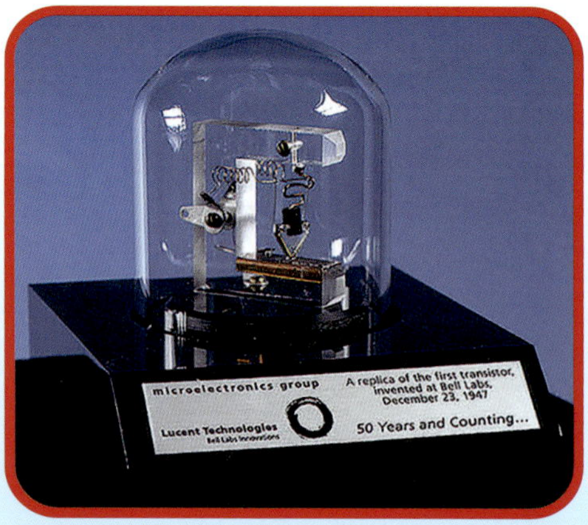

Lucent Technologies created this replica to commemorate the 50th anniversary of the invention of the point-contact transistor at Bell Labs in December 1947. (Image from Wikimedia Commons, public domain)

Computing's giant leap

The mid-20th century was a golden age for computers. In the early days, computers were gigantic machines, taking up whole rooms. They weren't very powerful by today's standards. However, the invention of the transistor in the 1950s changed everything. Transistors were tiny electronic devices that could control electric currents. They were much smaller and more efficient than the vacuum tubes used in early computers.

Thanks to transistors, computers started getting smaller, faster and cheaper. Jump to the 1970s, and another big invention arrived: the microprocessor. Microprocessors allowed us to load computers onto tiny chips. With this innovation, computers could process even more complex tasks rapidly.

For robots, this was huge! This meant they could now be programmed to do various tasks and even process information from their surroundings. The computer brains of robots became more powerful, allowing them to take on more intricate jobs and make decisions based on their environment.

Bottom view of an Intel central processing unit Pentium 4 Prescott type core, model 640. LGA 775 socket, 90 nm process, frequency 3.20 GHz. (Image courtesy Eric Gaba – Wikimedia Commons user: Sting)

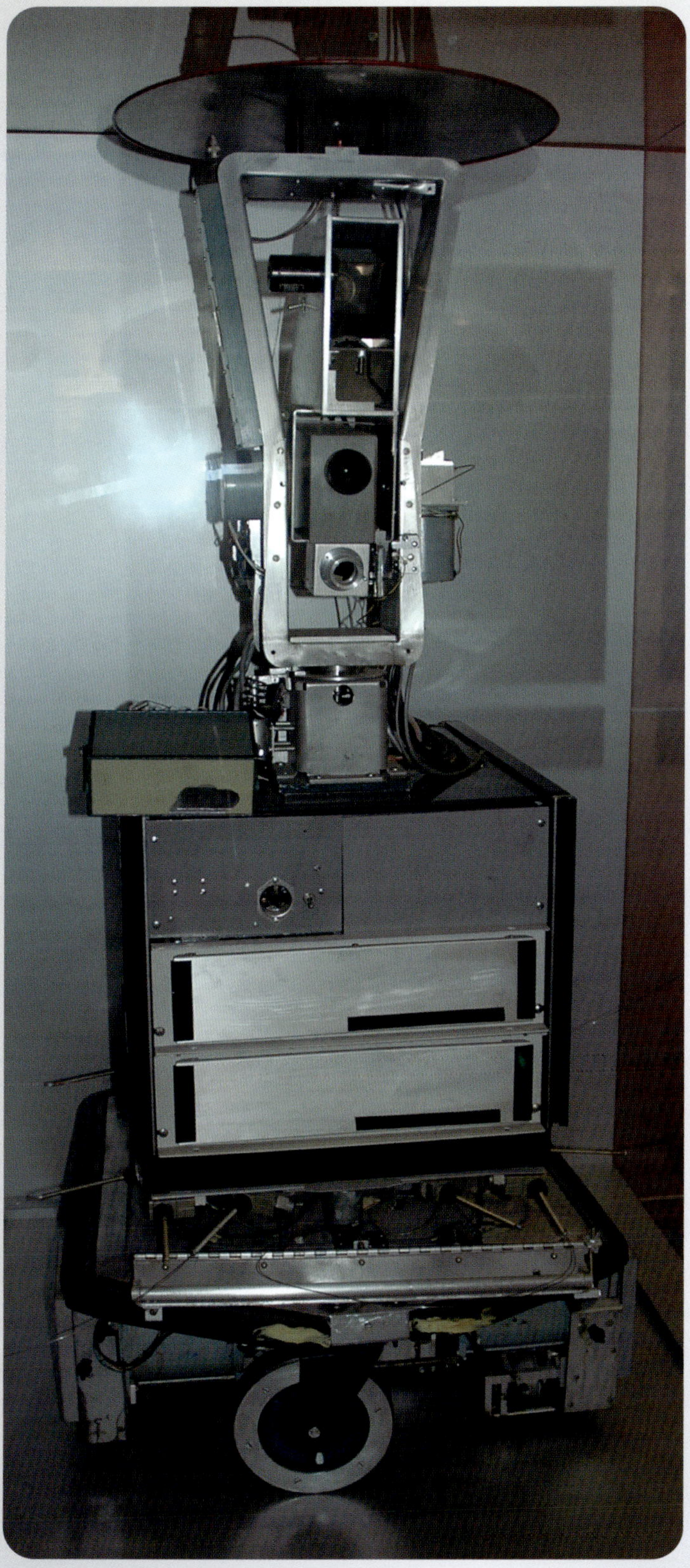

Fun fact

Meet Shakey, a robot built by Stanford Research Institute in the late 1960s. Shakey was the first of its kind, because it could make decisions on its own. If you asked Shakey to 'move the block onto the table,' it would look around, figure out where the block and table were, plan how to do it and even avoid obstacles in its path!

Shakey was able to do this thanks to a combination of technologies including a camera and optical range finder for vision, a radio link for communication, and bump detectors for navigation.

Its software architecture was structured into layers – a model that became influential for future robotics development. Shakey earned a place in the Robot Hall of Fame in 2004.

Shakey the Robot at the Computer History Museum. (Image courtesy Marshall Astor, San Pedro, United States, Wikipedia)

INTERPROGRAM
CSIRAC
17
16

Computers have evolved from massive machines that filled an entire room to something as light as a watch. Main image: CSIRAC ran an initial test program in 1949, making it the first computer in Australia to do so. Top: The Commodore 64, released in 1982, is considered to be the best-selling desktop computer model ever. Middle: Laptop computers have become faster, lighter and much more powerful due to advances in microprocessors. Bottom: Modern computers are now small enough – and smart enough – to wear on our wrists! (Images, clockwise from far left, courtesy https://collections.museumsvictoria.com.au/articles/2682, DanieleGay/Shutterstock.com, koya979/Shutterstock.com, Maxx-Studio/Shutterstock.com.)

Material magic

While computing gave robots their brains, new materials gave them bodies ready for action. Before the 20th century, materials available for building were heavy and not always durable. But new discoveries changed the game!

Materials such as lightweight aluminium and durable plastics became available. These materials were strong, yet light – perfect for building robots that could move with ease.

More recently, we've begun exploring soft robotics. Stretchy materials allow robots to be more flexible and agile. Their bodies can be more like yours and mine, meaning they can squeeze, bend and stretch.

Researchers have been getting creative with new materials. Some have made synthetic muscles using a form of silicone. Others have created silicone retinas that mimic how our eyes work.

But it's not just about being bendy and stretchy. These materials are adaptable. They can change shape with different triggers, such as heat, light or electricity.

This means robots can now be more responsive to their surroundings – sensing obstacles, recognising objects and even detecting a change in temperature.

3D printing: The key to a soft touch

Imagine your hand is made of metal. Could you pick up an egg without breaking it? Probably not, right? Metal is strong, but not very gentle. So what if we could make a robot hand that's not hard like metal, but soft and sensitive like a real hand?

In 2023, Robert Katzschmann and his team at the Swiss Federal Institute of Technology in Zurich made a 3D printer that ejects millions of droplets. It can create objects that have both hard and soft parts.

'It works a little like an inkjet printer that has expanded its skill into a third dimension,' says Robert.

Using the printer, Robert's team created the most human-like robotic hand ever. They even 3D-printed bones, ligaments and tendons.

'The printer builds up very thin layers using up to four different types of plastics or wax at the same time,' he explains. 'Each type of plastic has its own special features. To coordinate all these droplets, we use a laser and camera to scan each layer and account for any unevenness as the objects are printed.'

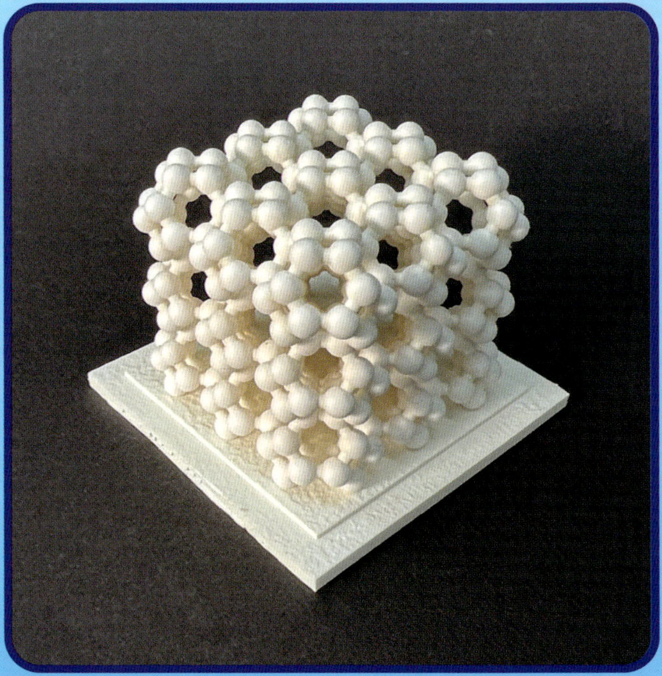

3D printing opens up new possibilities for creating complex shapes and structures, from walking robots to intricate molecular models, that would be difficult or impossible to make with traditional manufacturing. (Image by ETH Zurich/Thomas Buchner)

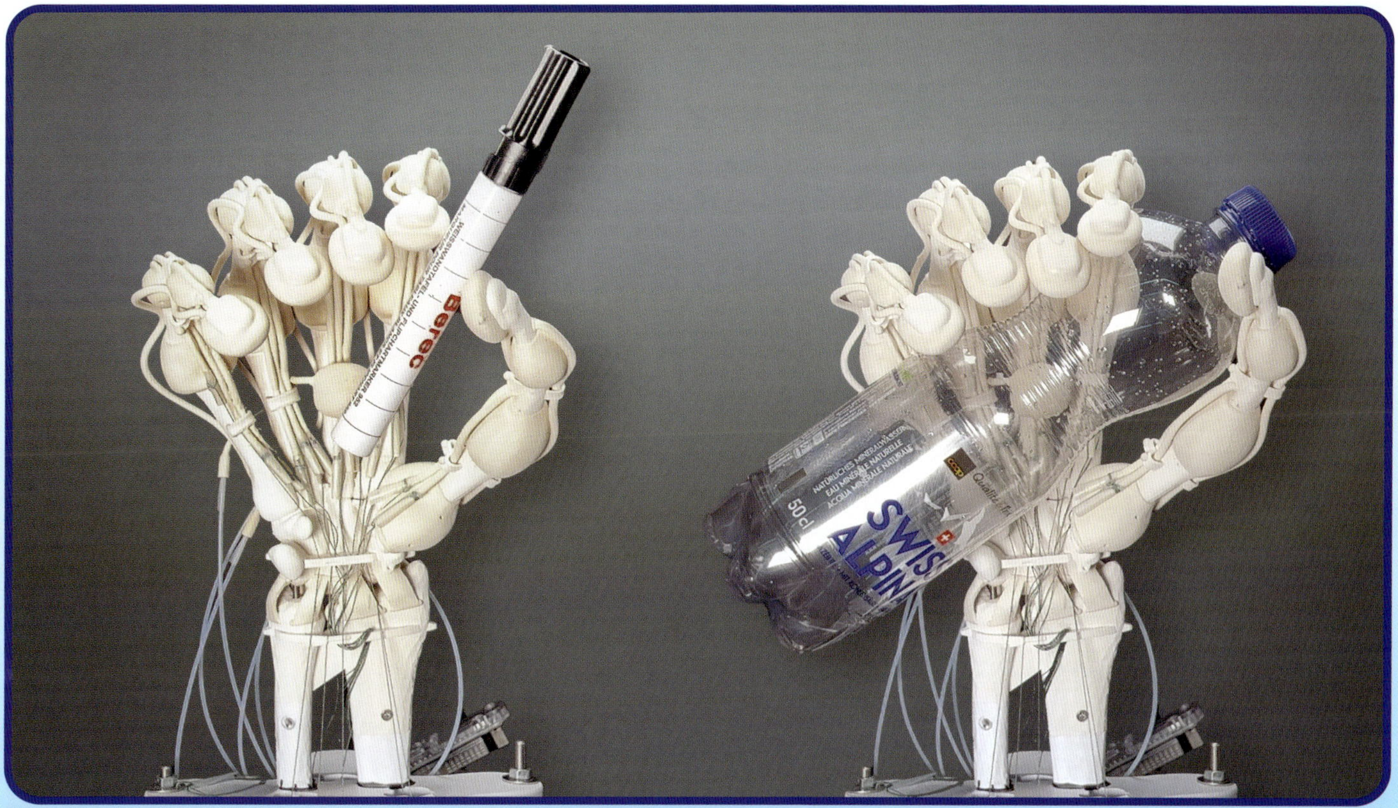

Soft robotics in action – this artificial hand can adjust its grip to hold objects as delicate as a marker or as bulky as a water bottle. (Image by ETH Zurich/Thomas Buchner)

This new kind of printed hand can do things that metal hands can't. It mimics human anatomy and can pick up delicate objects without breaking them. Imagine a robot gently holding a baby bird without hurting it. That's how careful this hand can be.

Robert is inspired by living organisms. Think about it: living things can be extremely flexible and versatile. Consider a cat. It can squeeze through the narrowest of gaps, climb up a tree trunk, or even twist in mid-air as it falls to land on its feet. Living things also adapt to different environments and have parts that work well together.

'These features of animals inspire key aspects of our robotic fish, walkers, hands and flying machines,' Robert explains.

His robots have smart, flexible electronics that allow them to interact with and understand the world around them. They can:

- move in lively ways because they are powered by liquids inside or strong electric fields
- handle objects both in and out of water
- fly and descend to gently pick up an object.

The brains of the robots that Robert and his team design use new models and learning methods to manage how the 'bio-inspired' robot works. This makes them good at moving around, picking up objects and observing nature.

'We also make bio-hybrid robots by combining living materials, such as biological cells and tissue, with inanimate materials, such as plastics, metals, or synthetic fibres,' Robert says.

These designs could lead to robots that get their energy from sugar and other nutrients, just like us!

Such robots could be far more energy-efficient than non-living, standard robots. Robert thinks bio-hybrid designs will eventually be able to take on a range of tasks that current robots can only dream of.

AI comes into play

Artificial intelligence (AI) is a clear game-changer for the field of robotics. It's hard to predict the possibilities that could emerge from collaborations between AI and robots.

Importantly, AI isn't just a concept in a lab. It's already all around us. From smartphones to cars, AI is helping devices better serve humans.

A branch of AI, called machine learning, lets robots learn from experience and data. This technology makes robots more adaptable, accurate and efficient at tasks such as moving, handling objects, and working with people and their environment. Using machine learning, AI is allowing robots to improve their capabilities and adapt to new situations.

AI will play a role in other places, too. It has the power to change how we create and test new materials and structures.

It can be used to predict how these new designs and materials will work in real situations. This helps make the development process faster and more effective. AI also allows for better testing and improvement before we actually make or use these innovations. This way, we can develop new and exciting things in a more reliable way across different fields.

As we make these advances, we must be extra cautious. Robots, AI and other technologies are tools. And like any tool, they can be useful or harmful. How we use them is vital. Ethicists are already asking essential questions about how we train AI and where we deploy robots.

We already find ourselves living alongside robots in our homes, workplaces and communities. That's likely to increase. We're heading towards having tools that can think and learn. This makes setting clear guidelines and ethical standards crucial.

Our primary goal isn't just to create advanced robots. We need to ensure these machines respect human values and safety. Educating ourselves, staying informed and talking about AI's place in our world can ensure that we harness its potential wisely. The objective isn't just progress, but progress that benefits humanity and keeps us safe.

As we integrate AI into robots, we're not just creating tools. We're building on a long history of innovation that spans ancient myths and today's technological marvels. Understanding this history helps us appreciate the impact robotics can have on society.

Ethical questions: Roboethics are critical

The field of roboethics deals with ethical concerns. Roboethics experts explore the complex questions of right and wrong surrounding the use of robots in our everyday lives. They think through both the benefits and potential risks.

People have different views on how and when robots should be used. Some think we'll see robots in every kind of industry. Others would like to see stricter rules and regulations put in place now.

Imagine a robot in your classroom. What tasks could it help you with? What challenges do you think it could create for your classmates and your teachers?

03

Say hello to the robots ...

So, now you know how cool robots are. Next, let's talk about how to recognise one when you see it. In this chapter, we'll also consider how robots think, adapt and make decisions. This is a quickly evolving field, with lots to learn.

Having insight into how some robots operate will give us a clearer view of how these incredible machines fit into our world and affect our lives.

Let's start here: Robots come in all shapes and sizes!

This is a robot.

And this is one too.

But perhaps the one you think of when you hear the word robot is this one.

Some robots are locked in place, while others roll around. Some have two, four, six or even eight legs and can walk. Some have wings and can fly! Others dive into the darkest, deepest depths of the ocean. Some robots are small enough to swim through your veins, while others are as big as a truck!

And you'll find robots all over the place: in airports, factories, hospitals and homes. If you're lucky, you may even have one vacuuming your living room right now. And of course, robots aren't just found on Earth – they are also in outer space.

So, how do we define a robot?

A robot is a smart machine that can sense what's around it, think and make decisions, and then do something based on those decisions.

So, essentially, robots do three things. They do them in steps, one after the other, in a continuous loop:

1. sense
2. think
3. act.

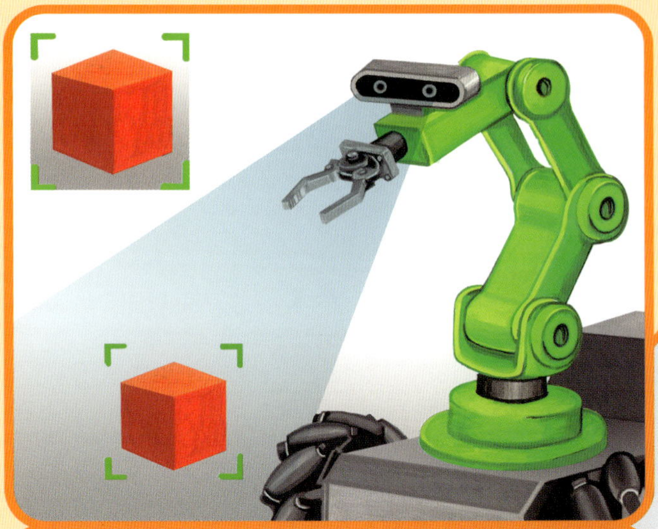

Sensing: How robots see the world varies significantly from robot to robot. It's based on the environment they have to work in. Do they need cameras for eyes, or would radar work better? Or maybe they need a spinning wheel, called a gyroscope, to help them stay balanced and know which way they're going. What about laser beams to measure how far away things are?

Most robots are equipped with sensors, which are devices that can pick up signals about the robot's condition and environment. The signals are passed to a controller to enable the robot to respond in a useful way. Depending on their sensors, robots can observe different things in the world around them and use their sensors to understand and interact with their surroundings.

Did you know?

The smallest robots can be the size of a grain of rice! They are called microbots.

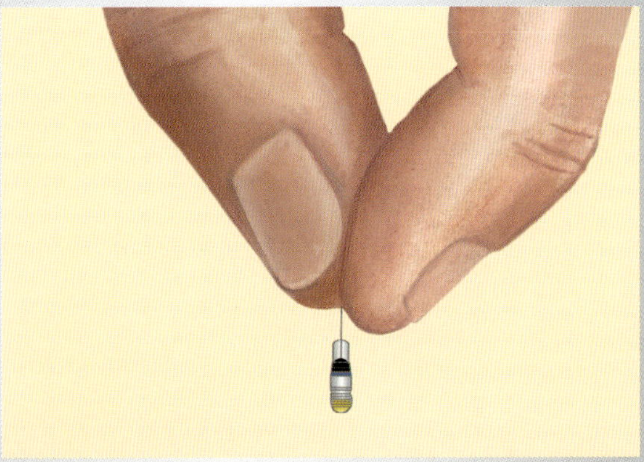

Thinking: How much processing power or brain power do they really need? When we ask how much brain power a robot needs, we're really wondering about the kind of computer parts it should have inside. For simple tasks, a small electronic circuit might be enough. Something like that can handle basic jobs. However, if a robot has to do something more complicated, such as planning a route or solving problems, it might need greater computational power. In this case, we could equip it with a multicore processor. (This is a more powerful type of computer that can think about many things at once.) And for really big tasks, a robot might even need a bunch of computers working together, just like a team of people would. Some robots may use specialised hardware or software to handle specific functions more efficiently.

Next, robots must 'think' about what action to take. And that's based on a computer algorithm. Algorithms are like recipes. Just like a cooking recipe guides you step by step on how to make a dish, an algorithm gives the computer step-by-step directions on how to solve a problem or complete a task. By following these rules and instructions, computers can perform everything from basic maths to complex operations.

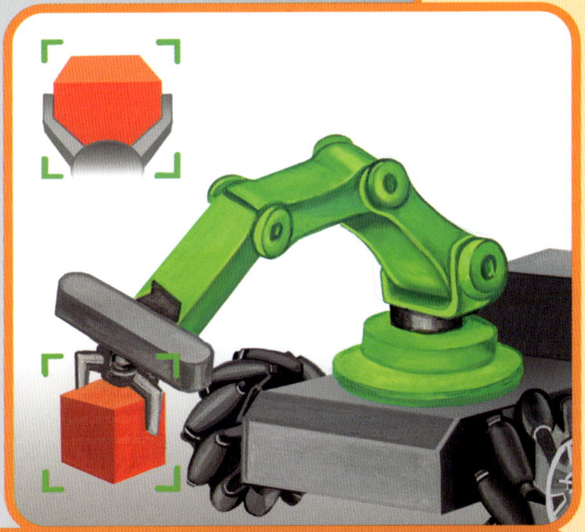

Acting: This is where our robots truly excel. We human beings are pretty good at certain things, such as walking. It's actually harder than you realise! However, robots have an advantage – they're not stuck with just arms and legs. They can be equipped with any kind of limb or mechanism we can imagine.

The devices that enable robots to move are called actuators. An actuator converts energy (often electrical energy) into motion. They can come in different forms, such as mechanical, hydraulic (using liquids) or pneumatic (using air). They act a bit like our muscles do, giving a robot the ability to move or change something. They can lift heavy objects, drive on highways, dive or even dance. Design and energy sources are important too! These elements ensure a robot is uniquely adapted – and very efficient – at taking on any task we want it to.

What next? Back to step 1! Once a robot takes action, it analyses its environment. Then it runs through the algorithm again and takes a new action.

Cleaning up the ocean, one spill at a time

Ocean spills happen when oil leaks out of a big ship or platform and spreads out across the sea. It's always an accident, but it has terrible consequences for fish, birds and other sea creatures. It's like pouring a huge bottle of sticky goo all over their home. Cleaning it up is very important, but it's also a really difficult job. That's where the Seaswarm robots could step in.

A carpet on the ocean

Seaswarm is like a carpet that floats on the water. Developed by researchers at Massachusetts Institute of Technology's (MIT) Senseable City Lab, it isn't too large, but is very effective.

The robot has a type of blanket made of a material called nanowire mesh that soaks up oil like a thirsty sponge. Nanowire mesh is a fantastic material that absorbs oil but repels water. It can absorb up to 20 times its own weight in oil, making it very effective for cleaning up spills.

One of the coolest features of Seaswarm is its ability to operate autonomously – it can navigate using GPS (global positioning system) technology and make decisions on its own. Plus, it can communicate wirelessly with other Seaswarm robots. This allows them to work together as a team to cover large areas of an oil spill efficiently – just like a group of friends efficiently cleaning up a messy room after a party.

Solar-powered heroes

The robot also has solar panels, which are like big flat batteries that get their energy from sunlight. This means they can work for a long time without needing to stop for a recharge. This is important because oil spills can cover large areas and take a while to clean up.

The MIT researchers think that a fleet of 5,000 Seaswarm robots could clean up an area of ocean equivalent to roughly two-thirds the size of Tasmania in about a month. This shows how powerful and efficient these robots could be in dealing with environmental disasters.

Best of all, the Seaswarm robot was designed to clean up oil spills without harming marine animals and plants – a big plus!

A project by the MIT Senseable City Lab, senseable.mit.edu/seaswarm. (Images courtesy Kris Krüg and Andrea Frank. Graphics by Adam Pruden www.adampruden.com)

So, can robots actually think?

To answer this question, it really depends what we mean by 'think'. Robots don't think the same way that humans do, but they can make decisions based on the information they sense from the world around them. This ability exists on a spectrum known as autonomy. Some robots can only follow direct instructions, while others can assess a situation and choose a course of action – sometimes with a little help from humans.

Let's look at a few examples to understand this better.

You might have heard of self-driving cars. These are often considered autonomous robots, because they can navigate streets, recognise traffic signals and avoid pedestrians. They make these decisions in real-time, using sensors and advanced computer programs. However, some of these cars aren't fully independent. Some companies have human supervisors monitoring the cars remotely. If the car faces uncertainty – like their camera images aren't clear or they've found a tricky parking spot – the car can flag the situation and hand control over to a human who helps it complete the task.

While the car shows a high degree of autonomy, it still works as part of a human–robot team!

Have you ever played with a remote-controlled car? You might have held the controls, where you push a joystick forward and the car moves. Turn it, and it steers the car in a new direction. There are no sensors, no decisions being made by the car – it's just a direct link between your hand and the car's motors. It's not a robot. It's a machine.

Later in the book we're going to meet robot 'dogs', such as CSIRO's own quadruped (page 48). At first glance, it might seem like these dogs are just being steered around with a remote control, like our toy car. But here's the catch: each leg has three joints, each with its own motor to create movement. That's 12 motors in total. Controlling all of them manually would be impossible! Imagine trying to make a robot walk if you had to manage 12 joysticks at the same time – no human could do that smoothly. Instead, the operator uses just two joysticks: one for direction and speed, and the other for rotation and tilt.

CSIRO's robotic 'dog' explores challenging environments using advanced sensors. (Image courtesy CSIRO)

The robot's onboard computer takes it from there, using sensor data to figure out how to move each leg, keep its balance, avoid slipping and step over obstacles, all while accomplishing its task. Even when a human is holding the remote control, the robot still does a lot of 'thinking' on its own. That's autonomy in action – local, real-time thinking based on what the robot senses.

Did you know?

Robots need to stay connected to understand us, just like a phone needs a signal. If you lose connection to a non-autonomous robot, they might stop doing their job.

For example, radio signals can be blocked by water or thick walls. This makes it hard for a robot to send information back to its team. But we do have some solutions. For instance, sonar technology (sound waves) can be used to direct underwater robot explorers, or to get them to come back to the surface to transmit their data.

Even robots that seem like they're just 'following orders' have some autonomy. A robotic welding-arm in a car factory might look like it's repeating the same motion endlessly, but chances are it has sensors to check whether a car door is actually in place before it welds. If not, it pauses. That's a simple decision based on sensing – and it counts as autonomy, too!

This is where it helps to distinguish between automation and autonomy. Automation is about machines doing the same tasks repeatedly, often with limited, or no sensing. Autonomy is about robots sensing, deciding, and acting – sometimes alongside humans, sometimes on their own.

So, can robots think? In a sense, yes. Many can process information, make decisions and learn from experience. But it's not a black-and-white answer. Instead, autonomy is a sliding scale, and nearly all robots fall somewhere along it.

Whether they're assisting on Mars, welding in factories, or navigating traffic here on Earth, robots help us do more by thinking – in their own way.

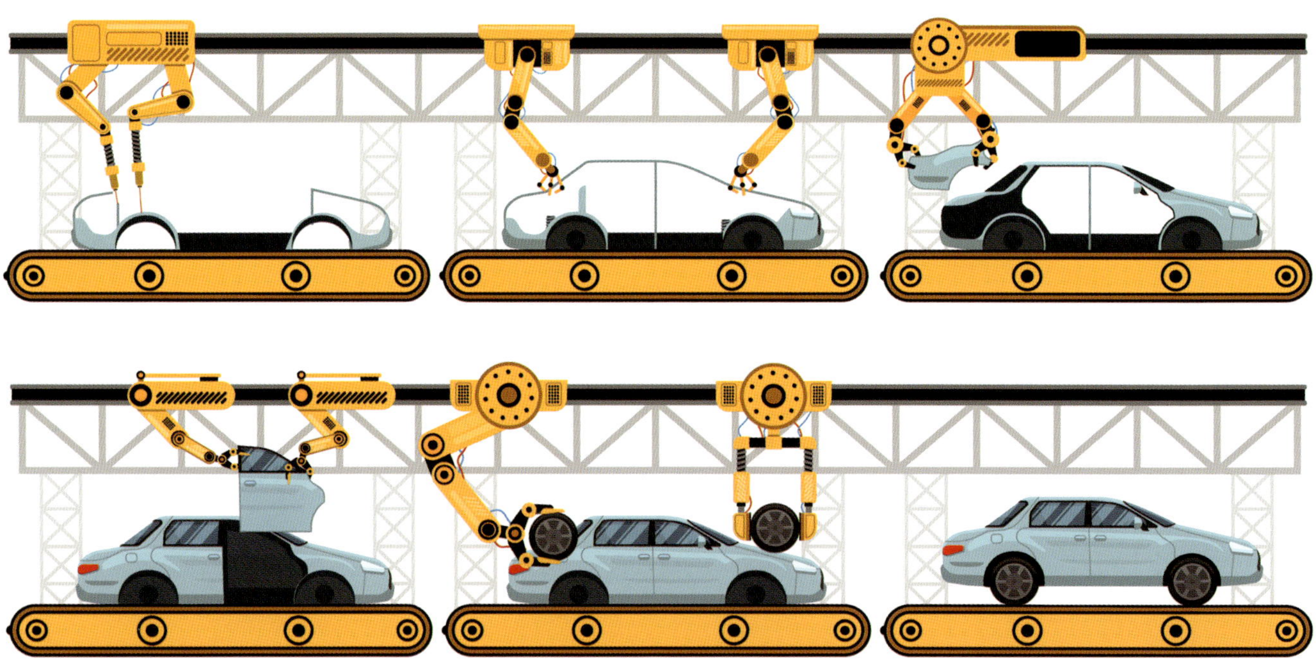

But how do we actually talk to robots?

Want to get to know your mechanical friend? Unfortunately, it's not always as simple as saying 'hi'. Many robots weren't designed to understand human speech (though that is changing now). Often if you need a robot to do something, you need to program it.

Programming is how we give robots instructions. Programmers write code that's like a detailed recipe, telling the robot what to do step by step. Just like learning another language, coding requires learning new words and rules.

Coding is a way to create smart, capable robots that can perform a wide range of tasks. For example, you can write commands to make a robot move, grab something or solve a problem. Using languages such as Python for simple tasks or C++ for control and performance of more complex tasks, you can direct the robot's actions precisely.

Controlling robots can also be like using a game controller or a phone app. For example, with a floor-cleaning robot, you might use a remote with buttons to start or stop it. You can even use a smartphone app to control it from anywhere.

Flying robot drones also work this way. They have a remote with joysticks, or you can use an app on your phone. This lets you direct the drone where to fly and see what its camera sees, all from your phone's screen.

Some robots do understand spoken words. And that's where things are really getting interesting. You've probably seen people talking to Siri or Alexa on their phones or smart speakers – that's voice recognition technology in action! And thanks to massive advances in artificial intelligence – especially the rise of large language models (LLMs) like ChatGPT – robots are starting to get much better at understanding natural, conversational speech.

Many roboticists are now exploring sophisticated human–robot interfaces designed to make our interactions as natural and intuitive as possible. Could robots recognise the expressions on our faces and be able to understand our feelings? Could we use our brain signals to command a robot without speaking a word? What about using simple body language or gestures to direct a robot?

The simpler we can make it to communicate with robots, the more we can benefit from their capabilities.

Ready for a robot pet?

Ever thought you would love a robot to play with? Some people already have one – because they own a robot pet! Sony's Aibo is a robot dog that acts like a real pup. Petoi Bittle is a robot you can build and program yourself. CHiP is another robot dog, and you can even find pretend cats and unicorns in the FurReal Friends series of toys.

Furry friends for life

You might wonder: how do you talk to a robot? And how does it understand you?

- **Speech recognition:** some robots have microphones to hear you and computers inside to understand what you're saying. When you say 'sit' or 'play dead', the robot hears it.
- **Natural language processing:** some robots are equipped with technology and processing tools to help them understand the meaning of words and the context of the conversation.
- **Machine learning:** some robots can learn from their interactions with you, improving their understanding over time.

Think about all the different kinds of families from all around the world who might own a robotic pet. For the pet to be able to understand them, it needs technology trained on many recordings of human speech and responses. This allows it to recognise patterns, understand what you want it to do and respond in the right way.

So, why do people enjoy having a robot for a pet? One big reason is that they're fun and interactive. Robots can do things that real pets can't, such as backflips or glow in the dark. Also, you don't need to feed them or clean up after them!

Adaptation in action

But how can a robot pet feel real? It's all in their design. We know engineers use motors to make the pets move and sensors to help them 'see' and 'hear'. This way, they can react to what's happening around them. Those equipped with machine learning may even learn from their experiences.

Dog-E: your new best friend? (Image courtesy Wowwee)

So, the more you play with them, the more they adapt to you – just like a real pet!

Will they ever replace your real doggo? No way. There's a reason we love our furry friends so much. But robot pets can be a cool addition to your family, offering a different kind of fun and learning experience. They show us a glimpse into a future where technology and companionship go hand in hand.

Ethical questions: Privacy paw-trol

Imagine if your robot pet could remember everything it sees and hears! While that sounds super cool, it also means we need to think about privacy.

If a robot can remember everything it sees and hears, how can we ensure it keeps our private moments, well, private? What rules should be in place to protect information we don't want to share?

04 Robots to the rescue: From dangerous to discovery

Have you heard about the three Ds of robotics? They refer to work you could describe as dirty, dangerous or dull.

An example of dirty work is cleaning up toxic waste. Dangerous jobs could include inspecting an underwater oil rig or entering a collapsed mine. And dull work? Well, you might argue that homework is dull, but a real-world example is factories that need the same tasks done over and over again.

The three Ds can be risky for humans. We don't want to expose people to toxic chemicals or risky situations that could hurt them. We also don't want them to get hurt just because they got bored and became distracted during repetitive tasks. This is where robots can excel!

Teaming up for safe rescues

There's another D we could add to this mix – disasters. In the aftermath of a disaster, rescue teams spring into action.

These teams are made up of people armed with the tools and expertise to rescue people. Sometimes, a rescue team brings along dogs trained to use their incredible sense of smell to find victims buried in rubble. The dogs can also use scents to locate a dangerous substance. However, there are still some things a dog can't do, such as tell us useful information – unless you can understand their barks!

Rescue teams often can't take anything for granted. This is because disasters transform the environment in profound ways. Entire buildings and neighbourhoods can collapse in earthquakes or be swept away by tsunamis. Floods can cause dams to burst and cover roads.

Once a rescue team is in place, thick smoke or dust can make it hard to see. Water can fill passages and fires can block escape routes. This makes it difficult to get to victims. For rescuers, this could mean getting lost or even trapped themselves!

While our rescue teams are skilled and brave, they're also human. They face limitations that can prevent them from reaching people in need. Some sites are places we struggle to access, let alone survive in. Think about the dark, tight confines of caves or the immense pressure of the deep ocean. You and I would struggle to see, move or even breathe in these environments.

This is where robots can help. They can survive environments with low oxygen, extreme heat and high toxicity. They can also navigate small, cramped spaces, sparing both human (and canine) lives.

Robots are good at helping us detect potential dangers. They can inspect and maintain equipment such as pipelines, bridges and power plants. By catching small problems before they turn into big ones, robots help prevent disasters from happening in the first place!

A search and rescue robot. (Image courtesy Engineer studio/Shutterstock.com)

Robots at work: Inside Fukushima's challenging cleanup mission

In March 2011, a massive earthquake shook Japan. It began deep under the Pacific Ocean, about 70 kilometres east of the Tōhoku region. The earthquake triggered tsunami waves, sending them racing across the ocean. By the time the waves reached Japan's coastline, some were taller than a 10-storey building!

More than 19,000 people lost their lives that day. Many times that number had to leave their homes. Houses, roads and buildings were wrecked. But that was just the beginning of Japan's troubles.

A disaster of nuclear proportions

The tsunami struck the Fukushima Daiichi Nuclear Power Plant, which was one of the largest in the world. At its heart were powerful reactors that used nuclear fission to make electricity. When the tsunami flooded the plant, it prevented its systems from working properly. The explosions and meltdowns that followed released dangerous radioactive materials, such as uranium and plutonium.

Radioactive materials release a type of energy called radiation. This energy can be really harmful to people and make them very sick. After the disaster, that radiation in some parts of the Fukushima power plant was so high that it could kill a human being in one minute! This made it too risky for people to spend time exploring certain areas of the damaged power plant.

That's when they decided to call in the robots. These robots had a very important job – go into the dangerous areas and tell people what was happening inside. How bad was the damage? Where was the radioactive material?

Designing these robots wasn't easy. They had to be incredibly versatile. They needed to navigate rough terrain where the earthquake had brought down walls and cracked floors. Some parts of the structure were underwater. Lumps of fuel and debris (deh-BREE, which means broken or scattered remains) were spread about. The plant's thick concrete walls prevented communication signals from going through – so, the robots had to be autonomous and work without direction from their human teammates.

Finally, radiation doesn't just hurt humans – it can make machines break down as well. The robots were built with radiation-hardened components to make sure their electronics and sensors could work in high-radiation areas for as long as possible. Engineers also gave the robots sensors to measure radiation, cameras to see inside the plant and arms to move things around.

Here are some of the robots deployed in Fukushima over the years.

- **Sakura** can roll over rubble and travel through water. It can carry equipment such as a camera to detect a type of radiation called gamma waves.
- **Scorpion** has sensors to measure radiation and a camera on its 'tail'.
- **ASTACO-SoRa** has two arms that can use tools such as pinchers and drills.
- **Mini Manbou** was nicknamed for its resemblance to the ocean sunfish. It was designed for underwater use in dark, highly radioactive areas, and can explore the bottom of flooded areas to search for fuel and debris.

The Scorpion robot from Toshiba sporting two cameras. (Image courtesy Toshiba)

Meet the team

Masaki Asano was part of the Toshiba team tasked with finding what everyone was worried about – the radioactive fuel debris in Fukushima Daiichi. Masaki has seen many robots struggle and fail in the extreme conditions within the plant. But he and his team are proud of what they accomplished with Mini Manbou.

'I felt relieved when we were able to capture images of what we believe is fuel debris,' Masaki recalls.

'Inserting a pipe into an existing hole of the primary containment vessel [the first barrier that contains radioactive material in a nuclear power plant] and then guiding the robot through the narrow pipe into the flooded vessel was tricky.'

'But my confidence in the skill of the operators who had undergone two months of intensive training proved fully justified.'

Toshiba's Kenji Matsuzaki led the operator team. He says the training schedule was incredibly demanding. They wanted to simulate (replicate on a computer model) the actual site, but they didn't know what the damaged structure would really be like.

To help them train, they placed all sorts of obstacles and created a lattice structure (a bit like a grid). The operator team then practised getting the robots through again and again.

'Thanks to the tough training using the mock-up, the objective of the investigation was achieved 200 per cent!' Kenji says. 'I am no longer troubled by a recurring nightmare in which the robot gets stuck and stops moving through the water.'

Science in action

Even with these innovative designs, it hasn't been easy going.

Some robots used at Fukushima stopped working or couldn't handle the tough conditions. Others got lost. Some couldn't communicate and got stuck. But every time a robot had a problem, engineers learned something new. This is a good example of how science works: try something, see what happens, learn from it and try again with new knowledge.

Cleaning up the Fukushima plant is a big project that might take more than 40 years, and there's still a lot to do.

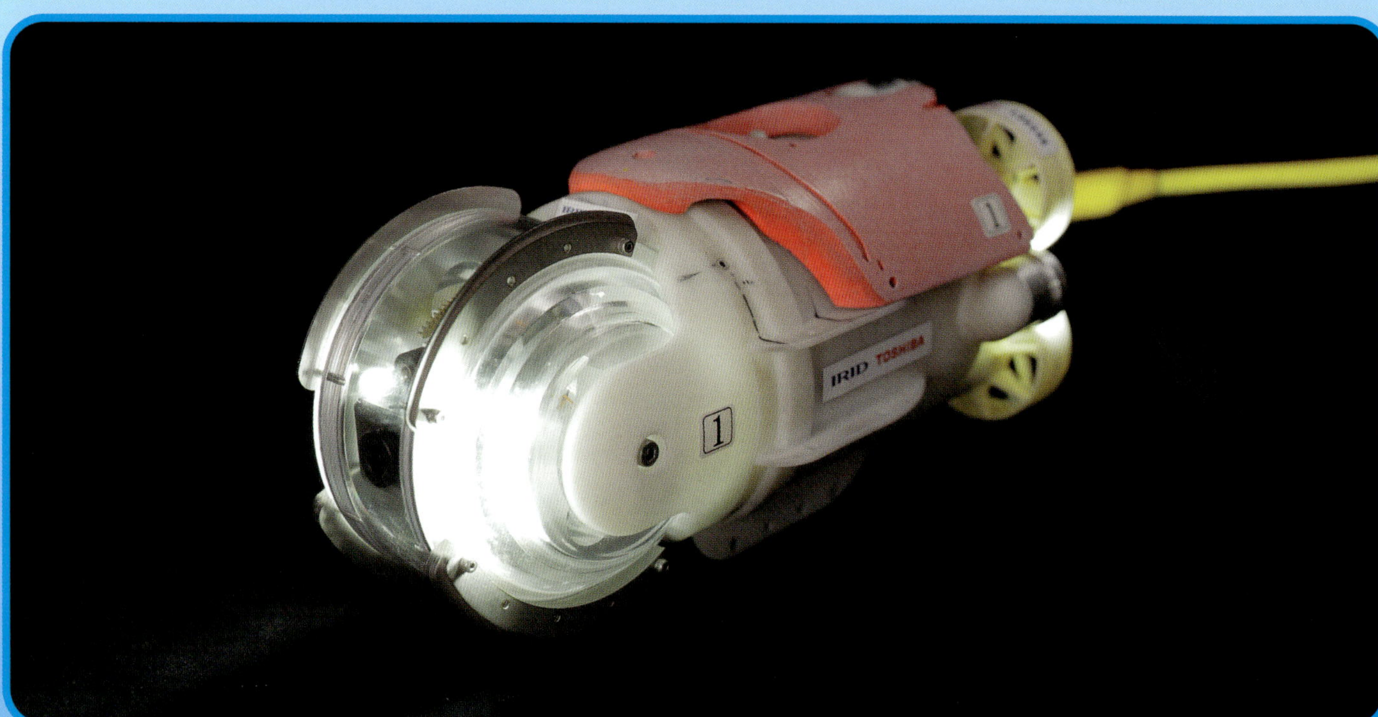

This robot is nicknamed 'Mini Manbou' because it looks a bit like an ocean sunfish. (Image courtesy Toshiba)

From deep seas to distant planets

I have another D for you – discovery!

Robots aren't just taking on tough and risky jobs. They are also amazing explorers, helping us learn more about our world and even other planets. Imagine being able to see the deepest parts of the ocean or walk on the surface of Mars!

Take the Mariana Trench – the deepest part of the ocean. It's so deep that the pressure would crush a submarine like a can of soft drink! But robots, such as the Deepsea Challenger, can dive there without any trouble. They use their cameras to show us what's happening in this mysterious place. They've found extraordinary creatures and unique habitats that help scientists learn about life in all its forms.

We now know that life can thrive under great pressure and in total darkness, far away from sunlight and the surface. This knowledge has helped scientists understand the origins of life on Earth. It has also inspired conversations about what life on other planets might be like!

And it's not just deep water – robots can also take us deep underground. In many countries, caves are so tight and twisty that people can't squeeze through. But small bots can crawl and drones can fly through them, making 3D maps as they go. These maps help us see the hidden beauty inside Earth and teach us about rocks and animals that live in caves.

Some of the coolest of all robots might be the ones that travel into space. Consider the Mars rovers, such as Curiosity and Perseverance, or Ingenuity – the tiny helicopter that made the first controlled flight on another planet.

These robots truly go where no person has gone before. And they feed our imagination, spark our curiosity and inspire our science. In the process, they're helping us answer some big questions: is there life on other planets? Is there water? Could we live there some day?

This view of NASA's Ingenuity Mars Helicopter was generated using data collected by the Mastcam-Z instrument aboard the agency's Perseverance Mars rover on 2 August 2023 – the 871st Martian day, or sol, of the mission. (Image courtesy NASA/JPL-Caltech/ASU/MSSS)

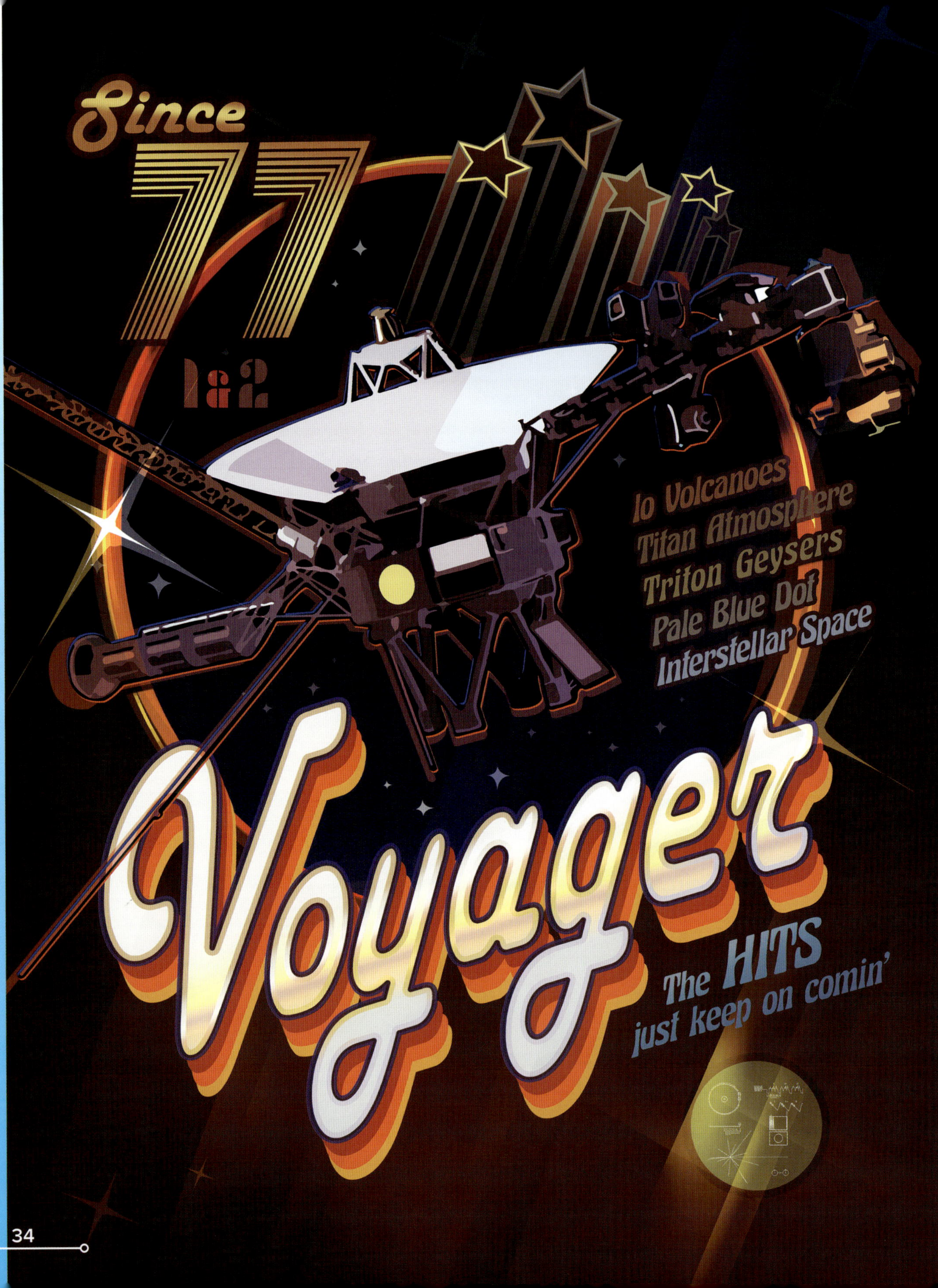
Since
77
1&2
Io Volcanoes
Titan Atmosphere
Triton Geysers
Pale Blue Dot
Interstellar Space
Voyager
The HITS
just keep on comin'

Did you know?

As of August 2025, the robotic space probe Voyager 1 had travelled more than 167 AU (astronomical units) from Earth. One AU is the distance between Earth and the Sun, or about 150 million kilometres. That makes Voyager the most distant human-made object from Earth – more than 24 billion kilometres away!

The Voyagers were launched in 1977. They've since helped us chart Earth's neighbourhood. They have discovered active volcanoes on Jupiter's moons, and been up close and personal with the stunning rings around Saturn and Uranus.

Voyager 1 is now in interstellar space, which is the space between the stars. But it will take another 300 years for it to reach the Oort Cloud – the most distant region in our solar system, thought to be home to a collection of icy objects.

On board the Voyagers are 'Golden Records.' These include greetings in 55 languages, music from various cultures and eras, and natural sounds from Earth, such as birdsong, thunder and the sound of a kiss.

If you were going to introduce humanity to the galaxy, what would you put on your Golden Record?

Opposite: Thanks to the twin Voyager spacecraft, music is truly universal. (Image courtesy NASA/JPL-Caltech)

Project manager Jean-Pierre de la Croix works on an autonomous pop-up flat folding explorer robot (A-PUFFER) during recent trials in the Mars Yard at NASA's Jet Propulsion Laboratory. (Image courtesy NASA/JPL-Caltech)

Meet Jean-Pierre de la Croix: Connecting robots and people

Jean-Pierre was in the eighth grade when he built his first robot. He used LEGO Mindstorms to get cracking.

'I started building different robots that would, for example, bump around to find their way around our house. Or they would chase light. That's when I think I caught the robotics bug,' he says.

After completing a PhD in electrical and computer engineering, Jean-Pierre joined NASA's Jet Propulsion Laboratory (JPL) in California.

Today, before NASA's robots travel into space, Jean-Pierre gets to have fun with them in an outdoor area called the Mars Yard at JPL. He knows space will be one of the most hostile environments imaginable for these robots. So, he first puts them through their paces here on Earth.

Say hello to robot teams

The space robots tested by engineers at the Mars Yard are known as rovers. The yard itself looks a lot like the surfaces of Mars and the Moon. It's filled with different types of land such as slopes and flat areas that the rovers can drive over and explore. This place is about as big as 12 tennis courts put together!

On a typical day, you might see rovers practising moving around, climbing hills and picking up samples, just like they would on other planets. Jean-Pierre and the other engineers at the Mars Yard can change the ground to test the rovers in different ways, making sure they're ready for their missions to faraway worlds.

For Jean-Pierre, one of the most important things is figuring out how robots can work together.

'I enjoy writing the software that eventually makes a team of robots move and collaborate in the real world,' he says. 'Seeing robots move according to the software that you wrote from them is about as exciting as it gets!'

Teamwork makes the dream work

Jean-Pierre loves the idea of robots working together like a sports team. He thinks about what would happen if we sent a bunch of robots to explore the Moon or another planet without people to help them directly.

He imagines the robots choosing a leader based on which one is in the best condition and has the right tools for the job. This leader would then give each robot a special task that fits what it's good at. As they work, each robot would find its own way to complete its task, contributing to

A Mars rover prototype is put through its paces in a simulated 'Mars Yard', helping engineers test its ability to navigate rough terrain and carry out scientific experiments before heading to the Red Planet.

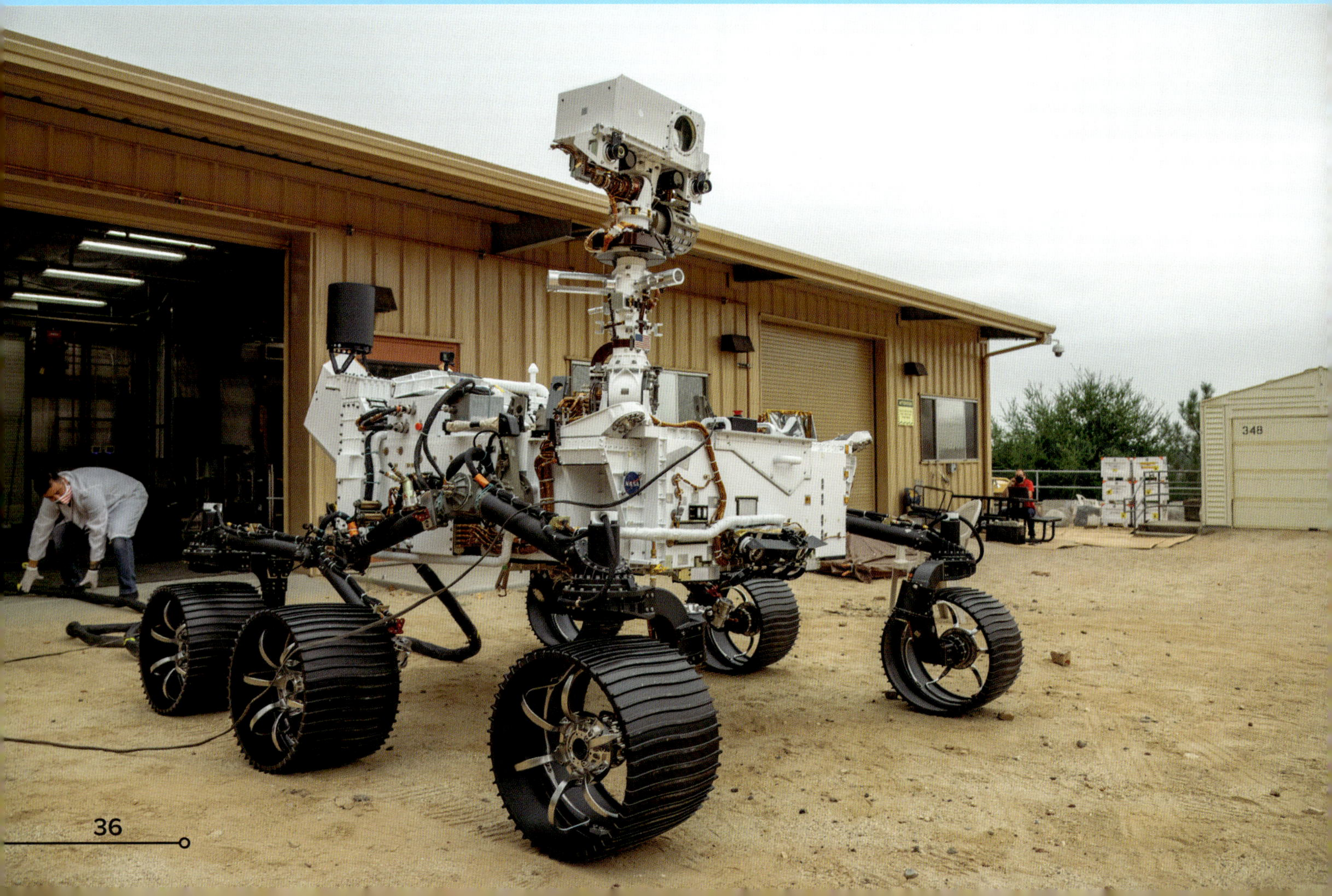

the group's goal. This teamwork is similar to how bees work together in a hive.

Jean-Pierre has used these ideas in his work with the A-PUFFER robot, a special robot designed for space exploration. His work at the Mars Yard helps get robots ready for their big journeys, teaching them how to work together to do better than they could on their own. This kind of teamwork could mean the difference between failure and success for space missions far from Earth.

His work has taught Jean-Pierre that robotics is a diverse field with many ways to contribute.

'Find what you enjoy, and keep exploring and learning. Also, find others to help you build robots – robotics is always a team effort!'

Want to know more about A-PUFFER? See page 75.

Ethical questions: When is it too risky for humans?

For decades, humans have risked their lives to go where no one has gone before. Our explorers have climbed to the summit of the highest peaks, circled the globe and walked to the poles. Today, we could send a robot instead.

Robots can go places that are too dangerous for humans, such as deep under the ocean or far into space. Do you think that's necessary? What do we gain – or lose – when we send a robot instead of a human being?

A Mars rover test vehicle tackles rocky terrain in a simulated Martian landscape, helping engineers refine its design for future space missions.

05 Dive into the world of roboticists

Robotics is a field of engineering and science. It involves the design, construction, operation and use of robots. It's the playground where science, engineering and technology meet innovation to create incredible robots!

And who are the people dreaming up these machines? Roboticists.

Think of roboticists as the superhero team-up of the tech world. Some people build stuff (mechanical engineers). Others write clever programs (software engineers). But robotics teams don't always fit a blueprint.

Depending on a robot's intended purpose and environment, different experts might pitch in.

- **A biologist** might bring insights from nature to inspire the design of a conservation bot.
- **A communication expert** might focus on helping robots talk to humans (and to each other).
- **Marine biologists** keen on studying the ocean floor or **astrophysicists** with their eyes on the stars will have different requirements to meet.
- **Ethicists** are interested in understanding how we can safely and ethically deploy robots in ways that protect people and their rights.

Roboticists are at work in every field you can imagine – from industry, manufacturing and laboratory work to medicine and even home automation.

GUS: A game-changer in wildlife conservation

One day, Gayan Kahandawa Appuhamillage opened his door and found a stranger waiting outside. The man introduced himself as Luke Townsend, a retired military captain who worked for an organisation called African Parks. He had a problem he needed Gayan's help with: animal poaching in Africa.

The brave rangers in Africa's sprawling wildlife parks put their lives at risk each day. The animals they protect are at risk from poaching. Poachers kill animals, strip their horns, tusks and skin, and sell these on the black (illegal) market for a hefty profit. This puts entire species at risk.

Poachers can be dangerous people who are willing to commit crimes to make a profit. This puts animals – and the rangers who protect them – in very serious danger. Luke wanted a tool to help the rangers, protect the animals and save lives.

Gayan relishes a good challenge. And he loved this one.

To start, they needed something that could help them keep an eye on the park. It had to be mobile and had to work even if it didn't have access to electricity. Gayan's answer was GUS, or Ground Unmanned System.

Gayan created GUS in part to help with conservation efforts. (Image courtesy Gayan Kahandawa Appuhamillage)

GUS hides in plain sight, keeping a watchful eye out for poachers. (Image courtesy Gayan Kahandawa Appuhamillage)

GUS's features

GUS is no ordinary robot. It has several features that make it perfect for watching over the parks.

- **Cameras** allow GUS to zoom into details that are very far away, or have night vision. This means GUS can keep an eye out for trouble, day or night.
- **A smart, sensitive microphone** uses AI to listen to all the sounds in the park. If it hears something unusual, such as a motorbike engine, it knows that something might be wrong.
- **A drone** provides eyes in the sky, taking off and flying around when GUS strikes rough ground. The drone can take pictures and record sounds, then send this information back to GUS.

With GUS around, the rangers have some backup. It can go to places that might be too dangerous for them. It can watch and listen, and if it finds something strange, it can alert the rangers. Gayan sent GUS to a park in west Africa, where rangers tested it in a program to help conserve wildlife.

Ethical questions: Who is in charge?

In rescue missions, robots can be invaluable teammates, helping people navigate dangerous or inaccessible areas. However, this raises important questions about a robot's role and autonomy.

Should robots always obey the commands of their human partners? Or are there situations where a robot should act based on its own judgement? For instance, what happens when a human operator and their robot are unable to communicate?

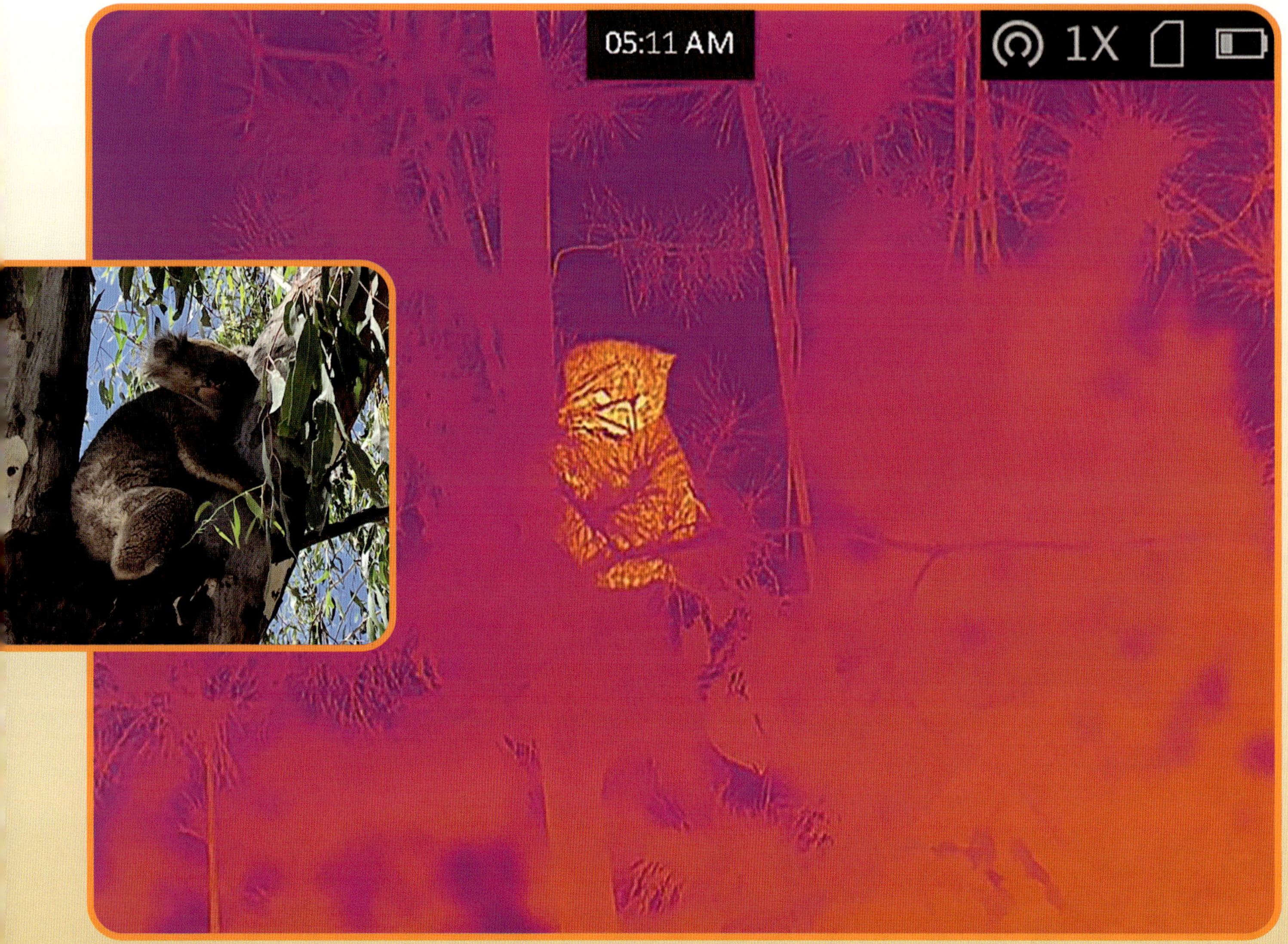

What a koala resting on a branch looks like through the thermal camera on GUS. (Image courtesy Gayan Kahandawa Appuhamillage)
Inset: Koala in a tree in natural light. (Image courtesy B. Melideo)

Can you spot the koala?

Now, GUS is ready for a new challenge – this time back home in Australia.

Gayan is working with a forestry company called PF Olsen. They've discovered koalas in their plantation in Hamilton, Victoria. The koalas live high among the trees and need to be relocated before the tree can be cut down for timber.

The task of koala spotting usually falls to people. Spotters have to keep their eyes trained on the branches overhead while walking in front of giant harvesting machines. It's a dangerous job – you really don't want to trip. However, it's one that GUS could do very well, all while keeping people safe.

To do this task, Gayan has equipped GUS with thermal cameras that can spot koalas in trees.

'If we detect a koala, we can mark the location and ensure the harvesting machine avoids that area,' he says.

With Gayan's innovative approach, GUS continues to protect both wildlife and people in new and exciting ways.

Amelia Luu at work with a robot. (Image courtesy Amelia Luu)

Meet Amelia Luu: Getting hands-on with robotics

Amelia Luu fell in love with robotics thanks to a bionic leg.

A bionic leg is a sophisticated prosthetic device that replaces someone's missing leg. It uses advanced robotics, sensors and AI to mimic the natural movement of the human leg.

Amelia watched as the bionic leg was fitted onto a dancer. During the video, the performer danced again for the first time since they had been injured.

'I thought it was amazing,' Amelia recalls. 'It was the first time I had ever seen anything like that. The technology encompassed both engineering, science and design, and it wasn't just a car or a bridge. It was something that helped someone in a really profound way.'

Her interest led her to study mechatronics, a field that brings together mechanical and electrical engineering. Amelia found the subject had many practical applications.

'I really enjoyed getting hands-on with robotics projects,' she says.

Helping with healing

Amelia has gone on to work on other cool projects, such as biofabrication. This field combines biology, chemistry and engineering to create living tissues or biological products. For her studies, she worked with victims of burn injuries.

When someone is severely burned on their face, one possible treatment is called an orthotic mask. To create the mask, doctors have to first build a mould. It has to be pressed firmly against the patient's face, which applies pressure onto the wound.

Creating the mould can be difficult for a patient who is already in severe pain. And not everyone could understand what was happening or why. Young children were often affected in this way.

Amelia had to test it herself to see what it felt like.

'It's a claustrophobic process,' she says.

Her solution was to create a photogrammetry rig. This is essentially a bunch of cameras that you can just hold in front of someone's face. It takes a series of photos and then uses software to build an accurate 3D model of the face. This digital mask can then be used to manufacture the mould. Ta-da!

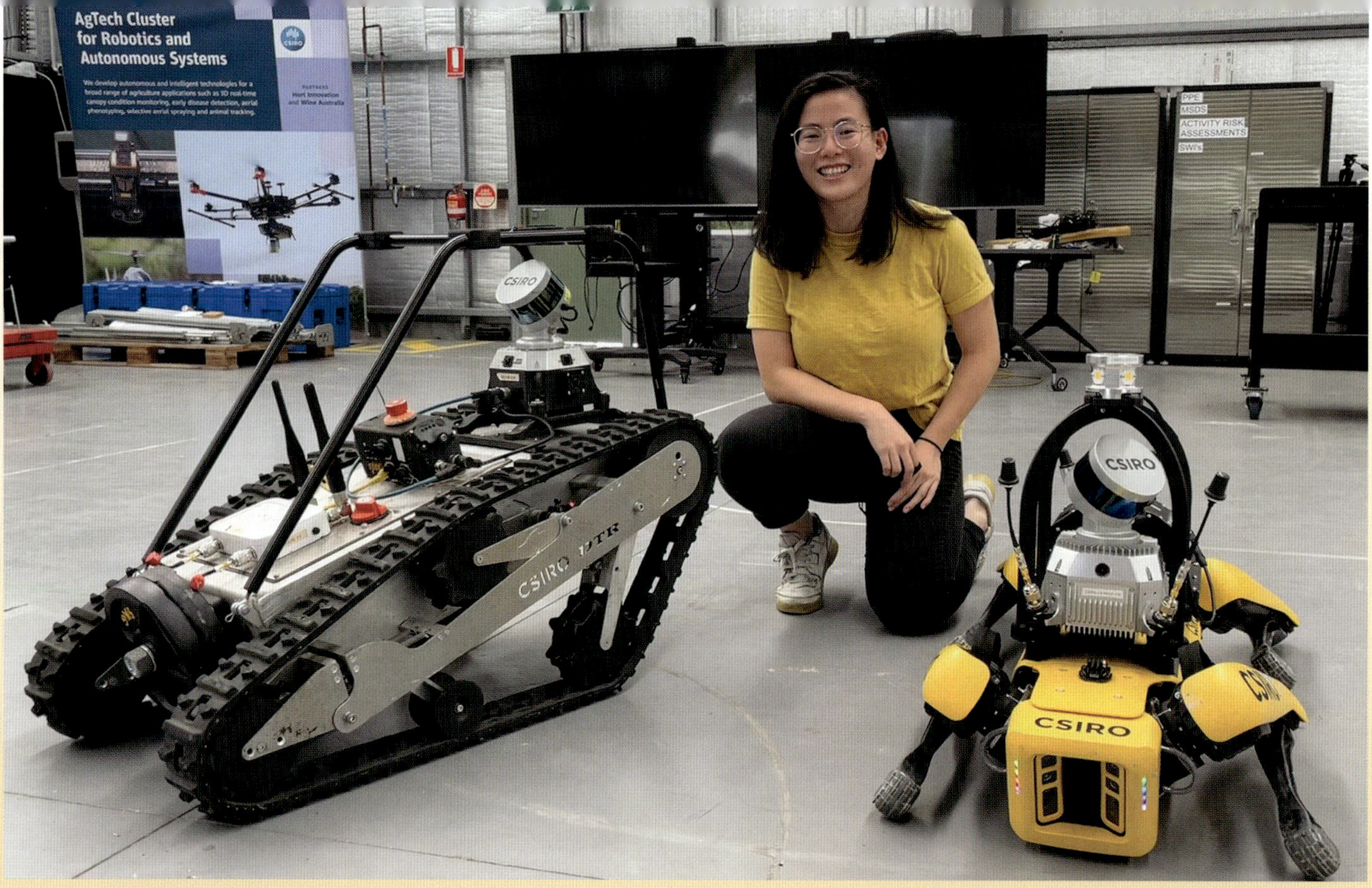

Amelia Luu at work with robots. (Image courtesy Amelia Luu)

Real-world innovations

Amelia went on to study how robotics could be used in manufacturing. One of her projects involved helping a company create artworks large enough to wrap around an entire building. She worked closely with the artists and producers to design a robot that supported them and helped them to get their job done to a high standard, with greater ease. She now works at CSIRO's Robotics group as a senior engineer.

Despite their versatility, Amelia doesn't think robots are ever going to fully replace humans. In fact, her experiences with robots have given her a deeper appreciation for people.

'Human beings are amazing creatures. We can do all sorts of incredible things. We're just unconsciously problem-solving and figuring out things all the time. And then we're making these kinds of micro-decisions constantly, in every kind of situation.'

In the end, Amelia builds robots to solve problems and help people. Her work shows us that technology can be a powerful tool for good, making the world a better place – one robot at a time.

Did you know?

Micro-decisions are small choices we make throughout our day. We may not even be aware we're making them. Yet, they can have a big effect on our lives! Think about packing your lunch – what are some of the factors you have to consider? They might include checking leftovers in the fridge, choosing the right-sized box, and deciding on which treat to pack.

06 Humans and bots: Spot the differences

Right now, humans can do some things that robots can't. But with the help of AI, robots are getting smarter. They might soon be able to learn and do lots of new tasks just like us! It's exciting (and very important) to think about what this could mean for the future.

More on that soon, but for now here are some of the ways we differ from our robot friends.

How do our brains work?

Humans: Your brain and ability to think and reason are the result of billions of years of evolution. Your thoughts and actions are deeply interconnected with your feelings, experiences and the culture you were raised in. The way your brain works also means you are a great generalist. For instance, you can use what you learn in school in many different situations, such as using maths when shopping or science when cooking.

Robots: Remember how we talked about algorithms? They're like 'recipes' for robots, guiding them on how to process data and act. Instead of truly 'thinking' like humans, robots compute based on these algorithms.

This is why robots are usually good at one thing. Non-autonomous robots in particular need new instructions to do new things. When faced with something completely new, they can get stuck.

AI could revolutionise this. By giving robots the ability to learn and adapt, we might see them become more versatile and capable of handling new situations. Keep an eye on how AI develops, as it could significantly change the way we interact with and rely on robots in the future.

Do we feel the same things?

Humans: You have feelings such as joy, anger and surprise. These feelings help you build relationships, make decisions and see the world in different ways.

Robots: Robots don't have feelings. Their actions are simply the result of programming. That's good for us, because they don't mind taking on the three Ds (remember, dirty, dangerous and dull?).

Ethical questions: Robots at the frontlines

In warfare, robots have the potential to change the landscape of combat, performing tasks that could reduce human casualties. However, this raises critical ethical questions about their role and autonomy in such high-stakes environments. Let's explore the ethics of using robots in war.

Should robots be used in military conflicts? Consider scenarios where a robot might have to decide between different targets or actions, or when and whom to engage in conflict.

Do you think it's ever right to have a robot fight a human? What rules should we put in place to ensure robots act ethically? How do we weigh the benefits of fewer human casualties against the risks of robots making their own decisions? For instance, what happens when one side can afford advanced robots and the other cannot?

Did you know?

Dogs have an extraordinary sense of smell. They can out-smell you and me any day of the week. This is because their noses can detect incredibly faint odours, and even identify specific substances. This makes them particularly good at tasks such as detecting explosives and drugs, diagnosing certain diseases, and of course, smelling butts.

Scientists are working on robots that have a similar ability. These robotic 'sniffers' will be equipped with advanced sensors and AI to sample and analyse the environment. It's a huge challenge, but if they succeed, it could revolutionise areas such as search and rescue, monitoring the health of the environment and diagnosing disease.

How do we learn?

Humans: You learn in many different ways, including by reading, playing, listening to your teacher in class, talking with friends, and even through making mistakes! You're curious and creative. You can dream up new stories, draw pictures and invent games. Your imagination lets you create things that never existed before.

Robots: Robots mainly learn when they are given new information or data. Autonomous robots can also learn through processes similar to trial and error. Their programming can adapt to and incorporate fresh data. They can adapt to new information and improve their performance through machine learning techniques, such as reinforcement learning. This means learning by trial and error.

Robots can also share what they learn with each other. With AI, some robots can even 'transfer' learning – that is, apply knowledge gained in one task to a completely different one. However, while AI can mimic creativity, it lacks some of the things that make us human, such as intuition and emotion. For now, at least, true creativity is still a uniquely human trait.

How do we act?

Humans: Our bodies are truly incredible. We can swim, climb, crawl and run. We know how to pick up objects or turn a dial. Our balance allows us to walk upright. And we live in a world designed for human beings. We know how to navigate obstacles such as steps, ladders, roads and doorways with ease.

Robots: Depending on their design, robots can roll, walk or even fly. Some have special arms or grippers to pick up items or press buttons. Others can balance on two wheels or navigate through difficult terrains.

However, they often find simple things – such as walking – quite a lot harder than we do. Robots typically aren't as adaptable as humans. They will perform best in the environments they're designed for – whether it's a robotic vacuum navigating a living room or a drone soaring in the sky.

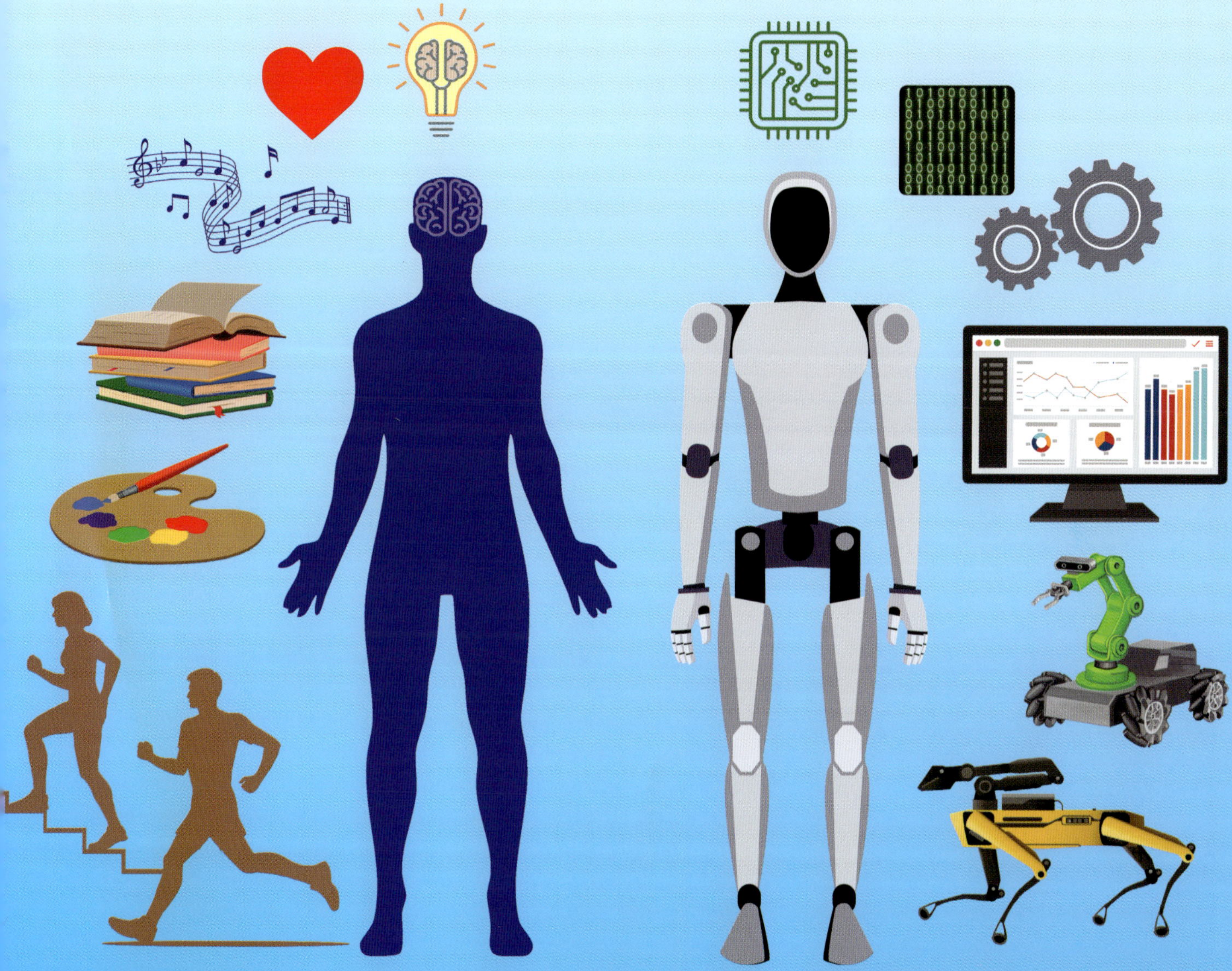

How NYPD's Digidog helped in a hostage crisis

In 2021, a worried man called the New York Police for help. He and his friend had been threatened by intruders with a gun and tied up in an apartment. He escaped, but his friend was still trapped inside.

That morning, the police arrived at the apartment, not sure if the bad guys were still there. To handle this safely, they brought in Digidog: a 70-pound (31 kilogram) robot shaped like, well, a dog.

Digidog is full of advanced technology. It has cameras and lights, and can send back sounds and pictures to the police from a distance. It can also see in the dark.

Thanks to Digidog, the police discovered the assailants had left the apartment and it was safe to enter.

Balancing safety and privacy

The New York Police have been using robots since the 1970s for risky situations, such as bomb threats. Jeffrey Maddrey, the former Chief of Department for the New York City Police Department, explained that the robot was a tool that could save lives – of both the police and the public.

'It's not going to be used for patrol,' he says. 'This is a lifesaving device. It's going to be used for hostage situations, bomb threats, counterterrorism situations.'

It's key to remember that Digidog wasn't a robot that made its own decisions. Rather, it was a tool controlled by police officers to check out risky situations from a safe distance. It had the ability to protect police officers by keeping them away from potential danger.

Listening to community concerns

But not everyone was so keen on the Digidog program. It also made some people worried.

For example, they were worried about their privacy. Could robots such as Digidog be used to spy on ordinary people just going about their business? Others feared that it might not be used in the same way in all neighbourhoods. Some neighbourhoods might see more use of robotic dogs. This raised issues of fairness and equality.

These worries about how new technology affects privacy and fairness are very important, especially in policing. Community members are also concerned about the cost of the investment. Should the police be using fancy technology when people couldn't afford to buy food in the city?

The Digidog project was cancelled. But in 2023, it was reintroduced by then-Mayor Eric Adams, a former police officer.

'Digidog is out of the pound,' said Eric. 'It is now part of the toolkit that we are using.'

What do you think of their decision? Could we get used to seeing robots in our police forces? There's no simple answer. It depends on the kind of conversations we have, the rules in place, and how well authorities address the concerns of the communities they work with.

Digidog on display in Times Square, New York, April 2023. (Image courtesy Lev Radin/Shutterstock.com)

Robotics systems in the DARPA Challenge had to be able to map, navigate and search underground environments. (Image courtesy Erin McColl/CSIRO)

Meet Navinda Kottege: Leading Australia's robotic charge into competition

They were going underground. Navinda Kottege knew he and his team had to be prepared for anything – narrow passages, ledges and sharp drop-offs. Not to mention smoke-filled areas, slippery ground and dripping water. The real kicker? They wouldn't even be there to navigate all this themselves. Instead, they were going to send a few robots.

Gearing up for the DARPA Subterranean Challenge

Navinda was going on a rescue mission – competing in the DARPA Subterranean Challenge. (DARPA stands for Defense Advanced Research Projects Agency.) Spanning three years from 2018 to 2021, this competition was a really big deal.

Elite teams from 20 universities in 11 countries went head-to-head in a task to build robotics systems that could map, navigate and search underground environments. The robots had to be able to do tasks autonomously (on their own). This included navigating the course and identifying key objects such as mannequins and mobile phones. They also had to communicate everything to the human teams back at the base station.

The robot team included quadrupeds, tracked vehicles, drones and hexapods for diverse tasks and terrains. (Image courtesy Erin McColl)

Meet the robot team

The Robotics and Autonomous Systems group, a CSIRO-led team, were the only Australian team to make it through to the finals. They had a great strategy, which involved choosing different types of robots for specific tasks.

- **Quadrupeds** have four legs for stability and mobility across various terrains.
- **Tracked vehicles** have continuous tracks, or a system of linked segments that wrap around wheels and provide better grip.
- **Drones** can fly and navigate on their own or take orders from an operator.
- **Hexapods** have six legs, giving them great stability and adaptability.

Each robot also had a secret weapon, Navinda says. It was a technology called Wildcat SLAM that helped it see and understand its surroundings all by itself.

This technology included a system called the Catpack, that let the robot know exactly where it was. It could also make detailed maps of the area without needing any help from people.

Even though the robots can work by themselves, they still need a person to help guide them. A member of the team told the robots what their big jobs were and changed plans when needed. They decided which robot should go on different types of ground, and set areas where robots shouldn't go. They chose the best places to put communication nodes, and decided the best times and places to send out the drones.

'Throughout those three years, we were learning continuously,' says Navinda. 'We learned lessons about the types of challenges we were facing, and we learned from mistakes we made. It was a very steep learning curve for us. But we took on the challenge.'

Together, they did so well that they brought home a silver medal for Australia! It was an incredible achievement.

From living beings to molten metal

Navinda has had an incredible career filled with interesting projects. This includes everything from designing robots for conservation efforts to underwater exploration to factory automation.

One project involved listening to animals in the wild, including frogs. This is known as bioacoustics monitoring. The next step was learning from what he heard. A frog call might reveal how big a population was, or the times when the animal was most active. But frogs are tricky customers.

'We got a bit frustrated, because we could hear the frogs, but we couldn't follow them,' Navinda says.

That's when he started thinking about how to make his monitoring equipment mobile. Of course, robotics held the key – particularly six-legged robots that could carry sensors and follow frogs around!

A few years later, Navinda completely changed the scale of his work – going from his tiny frog friends to improving safety in aircraft manufacture! He worked with a large aerospace manufacturer, using forklift trucks to move large work stands so they could safely rest against newly built aircraft.

Before Navinda got involved, these heavy stands were being pushed by human workers. The facility ran 24 hours a day, and if anyone made a mistake due to tiredness, it meant the risk of severe injury to people and damage to the expensive planes.

The sensor-based system Navinda helped develop was perfect for protecting people on the job. It could also work 24/7 without tiring, and work under different conditions.

Ready to go up a level

Navinda has let his curiosity lead him to solve many different problems. Today, Navinda is the research director of the Cyber-Physical Systems Research Program (Robotics, Computer Vision and Distributed Sensing Systems) at CSIRO's Data61, specialising in AI, robotics and cybersecurity.

Here, he's looking at pushing the boundaries with how we communicate with robots.

He wants to bring robots up to the point that we could just talk to them – without having to worry about coding or software. Another area of focus is helping robots learn from their mistakes and make better decisions.

Australia doesn't yet have a big robotics industry compared with some other developed countries. However, there are a lot of opportunities in fields such as mining and agriculture.

'In the future, I hope Australia will be able to address our challenges and become a global powerhouse in robotics,' Navinda says.

Navinda and his team had a solid strategy for the DARPA Challenge. (Image courtesy CSIRO)

07 Biomimicry: Inspired by nature

Nature's designs are clever, efficient and really adaptable. Can we learn from nature? Sure! Drawing inspiration from the environment in this way is known as biomimicry.

Robot design has been inspired by every animal you can imagine – from jellyfish to rats and even cockroaches. Why? Well, it's a clever shortcut. Through millions of years, plants and animals have evolved to make the best of their environment. Some of the most ingenious solutions already exist!

Take the gecko's foot, for example. It's a marvel of nature. It can stick to surfaces without any glue. It allows geckos to climb up vertical walls and even hunt upside down. Studying these little lizards has led to the development of new types of gripping tools in robotics.

Observing nature can spark great ideas for solving difficult problems. If we're trying to see in the dark, we might learn from bats. They use echolocation, a form of sound navigation, to find their way in complete darkness. Or consider rats, which rely on their sense of touch and whiskers to navigate and understand their surroundings.

And if we want to run really fast, we could study the unique musculoskeletal structure of cheetahs. Nature has solutions for almost any problem we can think of!

As a bonus, biomimicry encourages sustainable practices in robot design, as it's based on features that have existed in nature for millions of years. It's why we now have bots with arms like those of an octopus, or torsos like a snake's, or legs like a spider's. Robots even have the ability to swarm like bees.

And it's not just animals – plants provide plenty of inspiration, too.

We don't just look to the natural world for solutions on how to design individual robots. We can also learn how to best get robots to work together. Ants and termites are great examples of how little critters can achieve great things!

Copying nature doesn't just lead to smarter and more efficient robots. It also helps us gain a deeper understanding of our world. Even the smallest creature or plant has something to teach us about engineering and design.

Zee is a six-legged inspection robot. It carries a live-streaming camera and a real-time 3D scanning LiDAR. (Image courtesy CSIRO)

Did you know?

The Robotised Cherenkov Viewing Device is a floating robot inspired by a lily pad! It's designed to work in nuclear power plants. It has an underwater tool to monitor a plant's fuel rods, which are sealed tubes of uranium pellets. CSIRO made the software that makes it work by itself with minimal human supervision. The robot provides inspectors with a safe way of checking if the fuel rods are stored properly.

CSIRO team members with the Robotised Cherenkov Viewing Device. (Image courtesy CSIRO)

Getting inspired by nature's toughest insect

Cockroaches are geniuses at getting through tight and tricky spots. They can climb up flat walls and over any obstacle. Now, imagine how handy that would be for a robot.

Say hello to Omni-Roach. It looks a bit like a cockroach, with six bendy legs, a round body, and even wings that open up! It is about as long as a school ruler and as tall as a stack of 10 LEGO bricks.

Omni-Roach is based on a robot design called RHex, which is known for its flexible legs. What's really interesting about Omni-Roach is how it moves – just like a real cockroach! It can squeeze through gaps nearly half its width, clamber over bumps way taller than its knees, wiggle through super-tight spots, and right itself when it falls over.

The secret to Omni-Roach's skills is its tail and wings. The tail doesn't just wag – it moves up and down and side to side, helping the robot balance and fit into small gaps. When Omni-Roach needs to get through a really tight space, its tail helps it tilt and turn just the right way.

Yaqing Wang is a doctoral student in the Terradynamics Lab at Johns Hopkins University in the United States, led by Professor Chen Li. Their team designed Omni-Roach.

'Even the most advanced robots still often struggle to mimic biological movement in complex terrain,' Yaqing explains.

'By studying how organisms move, we uncover nature's fundamental principles and enhance our robots' ability to move.'

After lots of tests and tweaks, Omni-Roach got really good at tackling pretty tricky obstacle courses.

Yaqing and his team think the cockroach-bot could be very useful in real life. This includes checking out places that are too dangerous for people, such as buildings that have fallen down after an earthquake. Omni-Roach could even become an interplanetary explorer!

'Although the robot had a simple design, its understanding of movement physics allowed it to perform tasks almost as well as a real animal,' Yaqing says.

Yaqing Wang from the team behind Omni-Roach. (Image courtesy Terradynamics Lab)

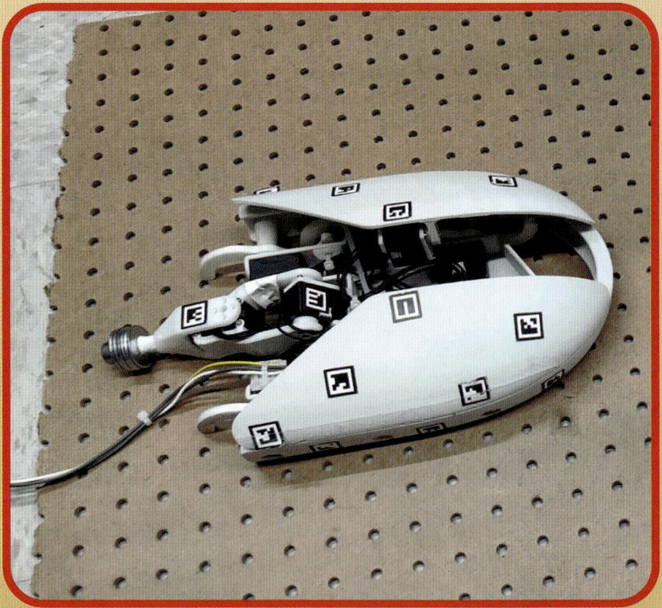

When it came to designing their robot, Yaqing Wang and his team were inspired by a very, very tough insect. (Image courtesy of the team from Terradynamics Lab: Jonathan Mi, Yaqing Wang and Chen Li)

The intelligent rat animat (iRat): A robotic marvel for neuroscience

Rats don't often become friends with robots – unless we're talking about iRat.

iRat is short for 'intelligent rat animat technology'. No, that's not a typo – an animat is an artificial animal, which could be a robot or a computer simulation. The word comes partly from '**ani**mal' and partly from '**mat**erials'.

A small robot about the size of a real rat, iRat weighs just half a kilogram. It is good at putting rats at ease because it mimics their behaviour.

iRat was designed in the labs of Professor Janet Wiles of the University of Queensland and Professor Andrea Chiba from the University of California. It's a powerful tool combining the latest in robotics and neuroscience.

Did you know?

Researchers can often learn things from simpler animals, such as insects. Ants, for example, have roughly 250,000 neurons (nerve cells). This is far fewer than a human's 90 billion neurons. Still, ants can complete complex tasks. Think about how they explore our big, big world, find food, and then figure out how to get it all back home. Ants also work together to defend their nests. Can robots be taught to work together like ants?

Making friends

Social robots help us learn about social behaviours. They can move around in an animal's environment and even get the animals to do interesting things. Sometimes, animals might be scared of robots and try to avoid them. But, if animals see robots as friendly, they might show prosocial behaviours towards them.

What does it mean to be prosocial? They are behaviours that often involve a sense of empathy, concern or compassion for others.

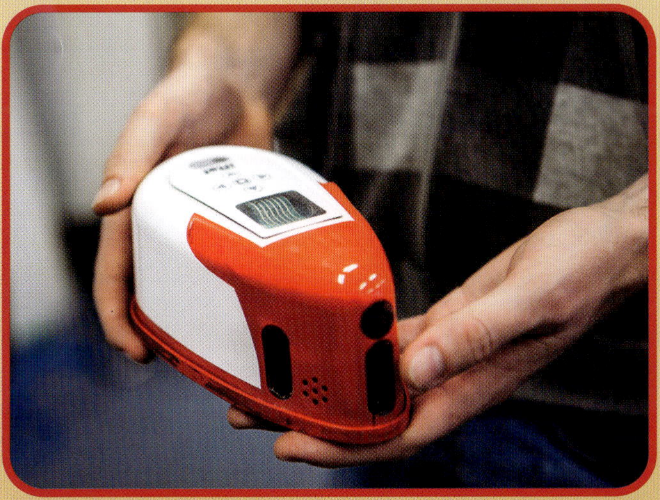

iRat is designed to look and move like a real rat! (Image courtesy Professor Janet Wiles, University of Queensland)

'However, we tend not to use 'kind' or 'empathy' when dealing with rats, as we can't know their motives,' Janet explains.

Instead, she and Andrea started using the word prosocial to describe the rats' behaviour without trying to understand why they behave in that way.

Many animals display these kinds of social behaviours. Rats, for instance, share food, help trapped friends and even help others in distress. If rats act like this with robots too, it would help scientists understand more about social behaviour and how robots can be used in research.

iRat is the key to this question.

Despite its small size, iRat is packed with advanced technology. It also has a differential drive, which means it has two parallel wheels that are powered separately, and one or more smaller castor wheels for support. Like the wheels used in LEGO robots, they allow the robot to move straight when both wheels turn in the same direction, but turn on the spot when the wheels turn in opposite directions.

Together, these technologies allow iRat to navigate complex environments, avoid obstacles, track its movements accurately, and process information when it comes to making intelligent decisions.

Navigating the maze

iRat is designed to move and sense its environment. Much like a real rat, it can navigate through mazes and respond to different stimuli (things that cause an action or response, such as sound or light).

Here's a closer look at iRat's features:

- **Navigation:** iRat uses wheels for movement, allowing it to travel at speeds of up to 1.5 metres per second, which is about as same as a human walking. It can also accelerate quickly to avoid obstacles, making it agile and responsive.
- **Sensing:** A wide-angle colour camera gives iRat a 110-degree field of view, almost like having eyes on the sides of its head. Proximity sensors at the front detect close objects, helping it navigate tight spaces without bumping into things.
- **Computing power**: Inside iRat is a mini-computer running a standard operating system, such as Windows or Linux. The computer processes all the data from the sensors and makes decisions in real time, allowing iRat to act quickly and efficiently.

A team effort

Over the past 15 years, many scientists and students have worked with Janet and Andrea on iRat.

'In my lab, researcher David Ball developed the first iRat, and PhD student Scott Heath programmed it,' Janet explains. 'Later studies included a smaller version, called the piRat.'

'The neural algorithms for navigation were developed in collaboration with Gordon Wyeth's team, called RatSLAM, and developed further by his student Michael Milford (now Professor Milford).'

'And Eric Leonardis [a former student of Andrea's] at the Salk Institute for Biological Studies is continuing to develop neural studies with rats and robots.'

iRat makes friends. (Image courtesy Professor Janet Wiles, University of Queensland)

Why is iRat important?

Scientists tested iRat to understand its capabilities. First, they got it to navigate a figure-eight track. Its brain-like system is inspired by a rat's hippocampus, which is a region of the brain associated with memory. iRat could use its 'brain' to create a map of its surroundings and determine its location, even in a complex environment. This research helps scientists understand how animals and humans learn to find their way.

In another test, iRat was controlled by a network mimicking how neurons in the brain communicate. It responded to a flashing light, showing it could process and react quickly. These studies help scientists explore how timing and sequences are understood in the brain.

The future of iRat

Researchers plan to make iRat even more lifelike. Future versions might include moving heads, whiskers and more advanced sensors, making it an even better tool for studying the brain. The team also created a docking station, though it hasn't been needed so far. This would allow iRat to recharge itself autonomously, allowing for longer and more complex experiments.

Ethical questions: Robots and the environment

Building robots takes a lot of materials and energy. We need to think about our planet and ensure making and using robots doesn't hurt the environment.

Do you think it's important to use environmentally friendly materials when building robots? Why or why not, and what materials could be used?

iRat is an exciting example of how robotics and neuroscience can come together to unlock the mysteries of the brain. By mimicking the behaviour and capabilities of real rats, iRat provides scientists with a powerful tool to study navigation, learning and cognition (the processes of acquiring, storing and using information) in a way that's never been possible before!

08 Robots in different environments

When roboticists design robots, they embark on a fascinating journey of innovation. Be it the Colossus in a cathedral (see page 61) or a rover on Mars, robotic explorers showcase the amazing blend of science, engineering and creativity that goes into robotic design.

Each robot must be tailored to thrive in varied and often extreme environments. Roboticists use many strategies to ensure their machines can navigate different terrains, including land, water and air. Robots also travel through the vastness of space, and even within the human body.

On land, robots must be stable and able to manoeuvre easily. Designers must consider varied terrain, from smooth city streets to rugged, uneven soil.

In water, aquatic robots or gliders face a different set of challenges. Ocean exploring robots must navigate strong currents and communicate effectively through layers of water, often over great distances.

In the air, drones and aerial vehicles must be lightweight yet durable, and designed to move through the air easily without bumping into things. This calls for smart guiding systems or navigation systems to help them understand the space around and move in all directions.

In space, robots need to handle the vacuum – that means there is no air. They must also deal with extremely hot and cold temperatures. Plus, they need to resist invisible but harmful radiation.

Robots also have to be able to send messages over super long distances, such as from Earth to Mars – all this while working with only a little bit of power! After all, they can't just plug into an electricity socket up there.

And finally, let's not forget to look in the mirror. Medical roboticists are designing robots that can work with doctors by operating on our bodies ... and even in them! From administering tests to actually entering our bodies, robots need to be accurate, skilled and careful not to do further damage.

Land, water, air, space and bodies: in each of these realms, roboticists push the boundaries of technology, blending creativity with scientific and engineering principles.

Did you know?

Radiation comes from various sources, including solar radiation from the Sun, cosmic rays from outside our solar system, and remnants of radiation from past astronomical events, such as supernovae (star explosions).

The robots they build are great at exploring, understanding and working within the unique challenges of each environment. But wait ... they also have some things in common! Here are some things we need to consider when we send robots to the rescue:

- **Autonomy:** Some robots are equipped to make decisions on their own. Others – remember non autonomous robots? – rely on human intervention. The more remote the area we're sending the robot, the more autonomous it needs to be.

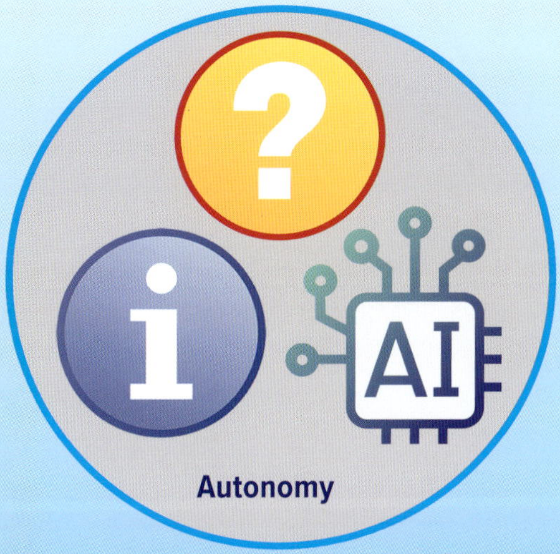

- **Adaptability:** Each robot must be adapted to its environment. This could mean anywhere from the vacuum of space to the depths of the ocean. We need to kit our robots out to deal with whatever they may find.

- **Sensors and communication:** From sonar to star maps, each robot uses a variety of sensors to help it to understand and interact with its surroundings. Robots also need to be able to communicate what they find back to us, or with each other when they're working in teams. Remember, there's no Wi-Fi on Mars or deep in the Mariana Trench.

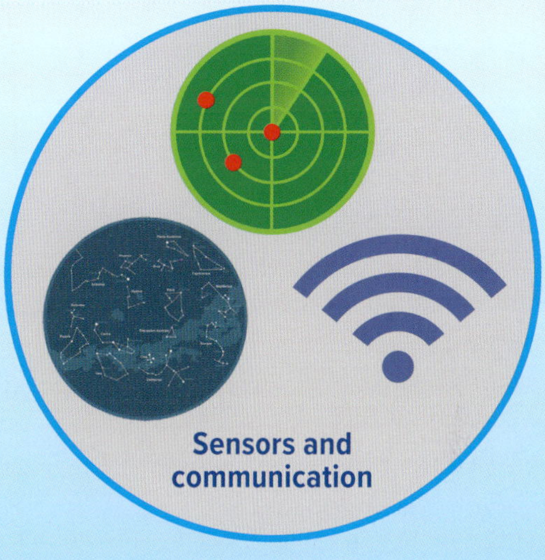

- **Energy efficiency:** Power sources can be limited in remote environments and power plugs may be hard to find. Can we use solar energy to power our robots? Or have them go into hibernation mode when they're not being used?

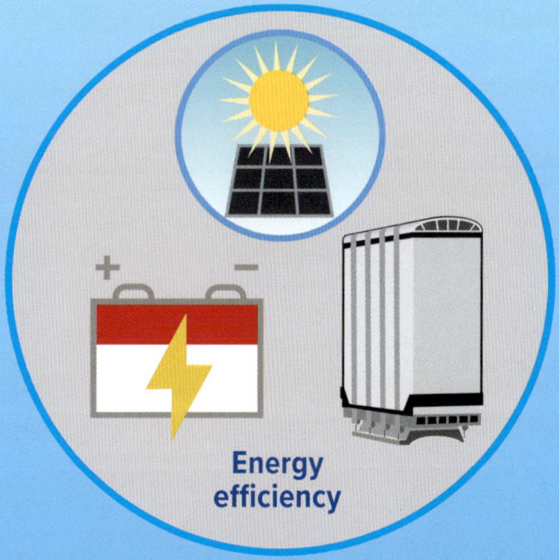

Robots on land: The rugged explorers

On land, robots can be asked to navigate the slippery slopes of a mountain or a deep, dark cave system, or anything in between. They need to be tough to navigate rough terrains and withstand different kinds of weather. Maybe it's freezing or hot or dusty – such changes in conditions can really affect a robot.

How they move: The first question we need to ask is, what does the landscape look like? Wheels or tracks will allow a robot to roll right through quickly and efficiently. But some need to have legs to climb stairs or ladders. What about sticky limbs? Those might be useful for a vertical surface, like how a lizard runs up a wall.

Finding their way: Land-based robots use eyes (cameras) and feelers (sensors) to see and touch the world. This ensures they don't bump into things. Robots on land can rely on GPS (global positioning system). This smart, satellite-based map helps us find out exactly where we are on Earth. Indoors, robots might make their own maps that show them the layout of a room or building – exactly what robotic vacuums do!

Challenges: Imagine a robot having to get through a collapsed mine shaft. Rocks could be piled up, slipping or sliding. The ground may be full of holes or have flooded bits. It's why they have to adapt and be able to navigate through a tricky spot!

Unique considerations: Robots must adapt to different types of terrain, such as mud, sand, gravel or rocky surfaces. Each type can affect movement and stability. If a robot topples over, loses its way or gets stuck, humans may have no choice but to leave it behind!

Weather-resistant designs are needed, because rain, snow, extreme temperatures and high winds can all damage a robot or reduce its performance. We also need to figure out ways to stay in touch with robots, even when they're deep underground. This is the problem with being under kilometres of rock – communication signals may not get through.

Ethical questions: Friends or machines?

As robots become more advanced, they can start to feel less like tools and more like helpers or even friends and team-mates. This raises an interesting question: How should we treat robots?

Some people think that as robots become more lifelike and useful, they should have certain rights, similar to humans or animals. Others believe that since they are human creations and don't have feelings, robots shouldn't have rights.

Should robots have rights? If yes, what kind of rights should they have?

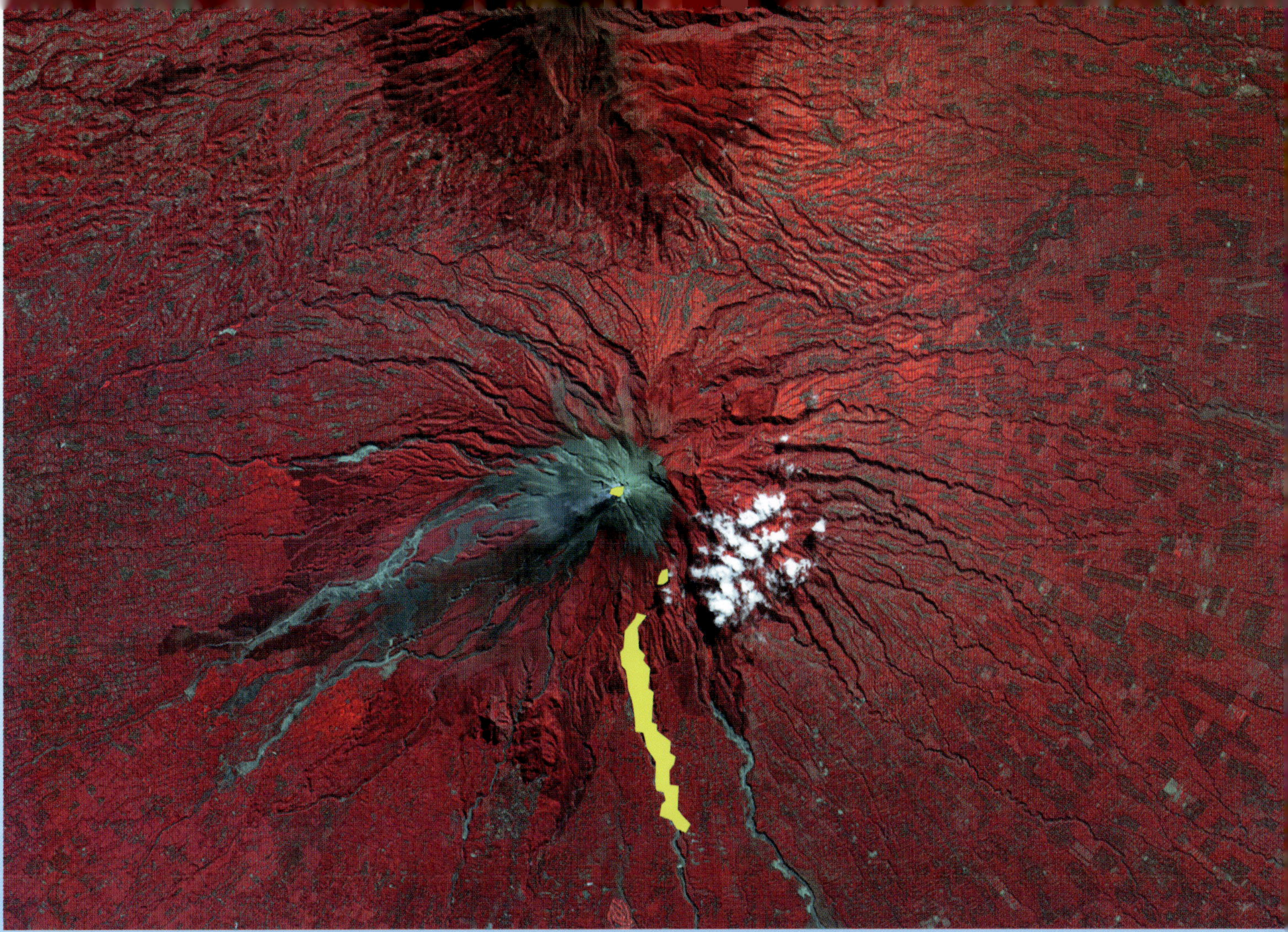

The ASTER instrument onboard NASA's Terra spacecraft imaged the hot volcanic flow that resulted from collapse of the summit lava dome of Indonesia's Merapi volcano, which erupted on 26 October 2010. ASTER stands for **a**dvanced **s**paceborne **t**hermal **e**mission and **r**eflection. (Image courtesy NASA/GSFC/METI/ERSDAC/JAROS, and US/Japan ASTER Science Team)

Braving the lava

Volcanoes are both spectacular and dangerous. During an eruption, a volcano shoots out molten rock, hot dust and gas. Volcanologists study volcanoes to understand how they work. One big mystery is exactly how magma (hot, liquid rock) travels up through Earth's crust and out a volcano's mouth.

Getting up close to a volcano, especially when it's active, is risky. It's so dangerous that some volcanologists have lost their lives trying.

Taking a peek inside the crater

Now, thanks to the people at NASA's JPL, there's a safer way to study volcanoes. They've designed a small, rolling robot that gives scientists a safe view from inside a volcano. VolcanoBot is designed to explore fissures, which are vents through which lava pours out. Vents are often filled with sharp rocks. Because conditions on an active volcano can change very quickly, it's dangerous to get too close to a vent.

VolcanoBot is an amazing piece of technology. It's agile, which means it can move around easily in tight spaces.

Dr Carolyn Parcheta was an important member of the team who designed VolcanoBot. She explains that it can currently go as deep as 30 metres, but that she hopes to extend that to about 100 metres soon. That's about as long as 3.5 basketball courts!

The researchers have developed three versions of VolcanoBot, learning from trial and error along the way. The biggest challenge was designing it to fit and manoeuvre in small spaces only 15 to 20 centimetres wide. Version 1 lacked sufficient ground clearance. Version 2's body was larger than the wheel diameter, preventing the wheels from touching the walls of the volcanic vent when it flipped over.

Luckily, VolcanoBot Version 3 worked wonderfully! Now, the robot can move up and down the vent's walls, and it can drive both forwards and backwards. Additionally, it can spin on its tether (a type of rope) when the slope of the wall changes.

How VolcanoBot helps scientists

Understanding how magma moves inside a volcano can help scientists predict eruptions. VolcanoBot helps them do this without putting themselves in danger. The robot can go into risky places and send back information and pictures. In turn, the researchers can warn people who live nearby to leave while it is still safe.

VolcanoBot is just the beginning. In the future, we might see even more advanced robots exploring volcanoes. They could go deeper, send back more data, and help us learn lots more about these powerful forces of nature.

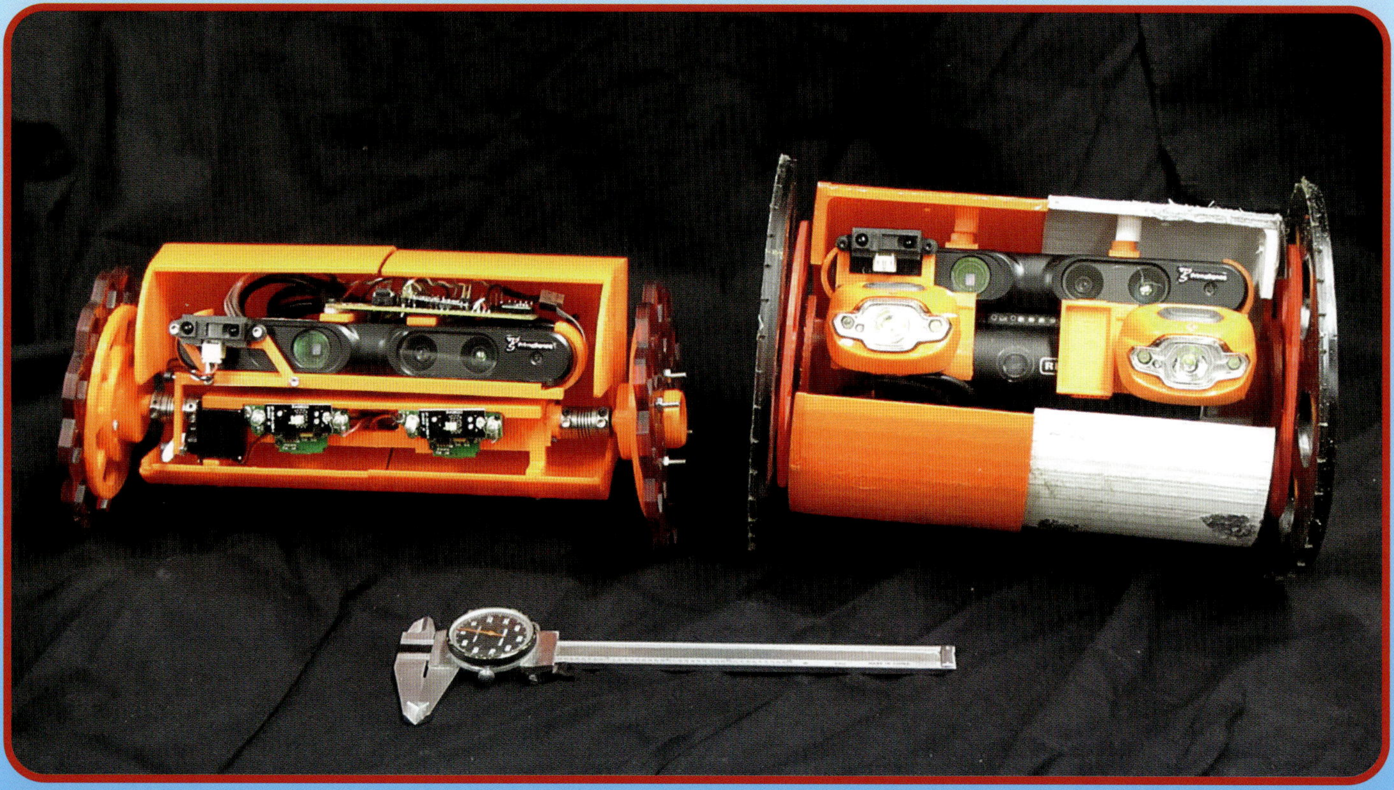

VolcanoBot 1 (right) and 2 (left). (Image courtesy NASA/JPL)

A firefighter unlike any other

It started with a plume of smoke on a clear April day in 2019.

The smoke soon turned into a raging fire. In the heart of the flames was one of the most famous and iconic buildings in Europe – the Notre-Dame Cathedral in Paris.

The cathedral had stood undamaged since 1163. The French people were proud of its vast interiors, stunning stained glass and majestic architecture. Over the centuries, various architects had each added their own touch to its Gothic design. Now, it was all going up in flames.

Taking the heat

The fire began in the attic and rapidly spread across the roof. More than 400 brave firefighters fought the blaze, climbing into the church towers to try and prevent its spread. Their mission was to save as much of the structure and priceless art as possible.

Enter Colossus – the remote-controlled firefighting robot. It has cameras, water hoses and the ability to navigate through debris and survive intense heat.

As the firefighters battled the flames, Colossus was sent into the heart of the cathedral. Its mission: reduce the temperature inside the building and douse the flames with water. It did this tirelessly. The robot's ability to withstand extreme conditions allowed firefighters to plan more effectively, without risking their lives.

Thanks to the combined efforts of humans and the robot, the main structure of Notre-Dame, including its two towers, was saved. The roof and spire were destroyed. However, the quick and brave actions of those on the scene prevented the complete loss of this historic monument – and no lives were lost.

Standing in front of Colossus, we can marvel at how a roboticist perfectly designed it to tackle the challenges of fighting a blaze. This introduces us to a fascinating aspect of robotics: the critical role of the environment in shaping a robot's design and function.

Colossus goes to work. (Image courtesy Manon.vermenouze, Wikimedia Commons, CC BY-SA 4.0)

Fountains of magma

The first time Carolyn encountered a volcano, she didn't even realise it. She was actually driving through a giant caldera – the large, bowl-shaped depression formed when a volcano erupts and collapses. The caldera she was driving through? Yellowstone National Park in the United States.

Carolyn still remembers her nine-year-old self being fascinated by the geysers she saw. A geyser is a hot spring that spouts jets of steam and water on and off.

'I was excited to think about hot magma below me heating up the water to make the geysers erupt,' she recalls.

Today, she studies lava fountains. In these fountains, molten rock erupts from the ground in a similar (but more complex) way to the Yellowstone geothermal geysers.

Carolyn studies data such as the movements and shifts within Earth's crust, changes in the landscape, and the composition of volcanic gases. This helps her understand a volcano's behaviour.

'There are many things to learn, and I personally love looking at the data to understand how magma moves through the volcano to reach the surface and then supply an eruption.'

Volcanoes in space

Carolyn's love of volcanoes has taken her to many places.

'I was fortunate enough to arrive at JPL as a volcanologist, learn robotics and systems engineering from the best in the world, and then carry those skills into a career position as a systems engineer for Mars InSight,' she says.

It turned out that Carolyn's work on Earth's volcanoes also applies to volcanoes on other planets. Some of these are ice volcanoes, or cryovolcanoes. Instead of magma, ice volcanoes erupt volatile substances (those that give off fumes or vapours), such as water, ammonia or methane.

'There are volcanoes and cryovolcanoes on many worlds. My interest in how magma (and cryomagma) move through a planet's crust spans various space exploration topics and locations, such as Venus, Mars, Io, Enceladus and Europa,' Carolyn says.

During her time at JPL, people were interested in adapting VolcanoBot for exploring icy moons such as

Carolyn Parcheta from NASA's Jet Propulsion Laboratory plans to take VolcanoBot to explore Hawaii's Kilauea volcano. (Image courtesy NASA/JPL)

NASA's Cassini spacecraft captured this view as it neared icy Enceladus for its closest-ever dive past the moon's active south-polar region. The view shows heavily cratered northern latitudes at top, changing to fractured, wrinkled terrain. (Image courtesy NASA/JPL-Caltech/Space Science Institute)

Enceladus, which orbits Saturn. On Enceladus, cryomagma erupts in jets from cracks, similar to lava fountains on Earth – but bigger.

The robot currently hangs from a tether in volcanic vents, relying on Earth's gravity. It needs modifications to work properly in the microgravity of space, where objects feel almost weightless. In this environment, objects float, making it harder for robots to move and stay stable.

Carolyn's experience exploring lava tubes helps her identify potential shelter locations on the Moon and Mars for future missions. Shelters will provide safe places for astronauts, protecting them from harsh conditions, such as radiation and extreme temperatures – much like the natural shelters she studies here on Earth.

Bringing many hobbies together

Carolyn has many interests outside volcanoes, but she finds they all help her connect the dots in scientific data in unexpected ways – and vice versa.

Making patchwork quilts taught her to see the bigger picture from many small pieces, and bookbinding taught her to be efficient through repetition. Painting showed her the importance of step-by-step progress, while carpentry highlighted how connections can affect structural integrity and how different methods of joining pieces can influence the final product's strength. Cooking taught her about balancing ingredients, which she finds similar to tweaking scientific methods. And when she looks at the textures of food, she sees resemblances to volcanic processes.

Paving your own path

When Carolyn first said she wanted to map a volcanic fissure, many people thought it was impossible ... until the robot was built.

'Sometimes you might be the only one who can see the path forward,' she says. 'You may have the solution that no one else has thought of yet – and you should pursue that with all your passion.'

'Create the tools you need to do the cutting edge (and often fundamental) science and engineering that captures your interest. You'll be amazed at the things you'll learn – some of those things will be the first time anyone in our history learns them! And you'll get to share that new knowledge or engineering tool with the world.'

'Don't wait for the path to appear before you ... sometimes you have to go out and pave the path yourself. And that is the kind of exploration I think is most worth pursuing.'

Robots in water: Sink, swim or float?

Underwater robots can be put to work in rivers, lakes and oceans. Some just float at the top. Others are like mini-submarines, reaching depths that humans can't.

How they move: Propellers or little jets help them swim through water, gliding past fish and coral reefs. Robots on the surface might use motors or sails.

Finding their way: GPS doesn't work underwater. So these robots use sonar, which stands for **so**und **na**vigation **r**anging. Sonar technology uses sound to see things in water, which is often murky or really deep and dark. Although light doesn't travel far underwater, sound waves do. So, sonar helps us 'see' things underwater that we can't see with our eyes.

Challenges: The deeper robots go, the more water pushes on them. Imagine a stack of heavy books on your back. You would need to be super strong to handle this pressure without going 'squish' – and so do underwater robots!

Salty ocean water is also corrosive. It can 'eat' metal robot bodies, weakening them. To survive, these robots need effective waterproof designs.

Unique considerations: Moving around underwater is different from on land or in the air, because of water currents and resistance. Robots need to be able to move efficiently and be stable enough to perform tasks even when currents are pushing against them.

And the deeper you go underwater, the darker it gets. Sunlight doesn't reach the depths of the ocean, or even some of our deepest lakes. Robots need their own lights to see, or use sensors that don't need light to work.

Lionfish hunters: Watch out for that harpoon!

People in Florida and Bermuda have plenty of reasons to dislike lionfish.

For starters, lionfish are invasive, meaning they don't belong there. Originally from the South Pacific, they have spread to water in places such as Florida, where they have no natural predators. This lets them grow in huge numbers.

Another reason is their appetite. Lionfish eat a lot and aren't picky, so they compete with local fish for food. They're also tough to catch, because they don't go after traditional fishing lures, and are difficult to snag in nets.

But the really big problem is there are just too many of them. This has a terrible impact on the environment. Certain regions can be so densely populated that you might find hundreds of lionfish within an area as small as a soccer pitch. That's bad news for the local marine life, especially smaller fish and crustaceans. Lionfish outcompete them for food and space, which can damage coral reefs and disrupt the whole ecosystem.

Researchers from Oregon State University found that the presence of a single lionfish can drive down a coral reef's diversity (the number of different species) by nearly 80 per cent.

Harpoon gun, anyone?

To combat this, people have tried various methods, including fishing competitions and hunting them using diving gear.

Despite the valiant efforts of divers, some lionfish have remained far out of reach. For instance, 2016 surveys showed that lionfish were present around the edge of Bermuda at depths as great as 300 metres – far below where humans could go using dive gear.

The answer to this dilemma was Reef Sweeper – a robot known as a remotely operated vehicle (ROV). Designed by a Bermuda-based company, Atlantic Lionshare, it uses a harpoon gun to exterminate its fierce target. Reef Sweeper was designed to go deep below the water's surface. An operator controls it from the surface using a joystick.

Gavin Hunter from Atlantic Lionshare describes lionfish as 'a beautiful fish in beautiful locations doing ugly things.'

'We are working hard to protect the environment from this highly damaging species, which decimates the reefs as it eats its way through many local species,' he says.

Their ROV can catch many lionfish in one go, helping to control their population. This helps the environment and protects other vulnerable marine creatures.

Gavin explains they're now integrating AI into Reef Sweeper to help it locate and identify fish. AI will also help map out the best route for the robot to take across the ocean floor. This means it will soon be able to work independently!

As an unexpected bonus, the captured lionfish are edible! So, the robot is not just keeping the ocean healthy – our dinner plates could benefit, too.

Reef Sweeper catches many lionfish in one go, helping to control the population of this invasive species. (Image courtesy Atlantic Lionshare)

SuBastain, the ROV, dove to 4,500 metres, documenting more than 100 previously unseen species.
(Image courtesy Schmidt Ocean Institute, CC BY-SA 4.0)

Discovering deep-sea secrets

Whether they're underwater or on land, mountains are challenging to explore – unless you have a robot who can help.

An international team of scientists recently embarked on a fascinating expedition to explore the seamounts (underwater mountains) off the coast of Chile in South America. The star of the expedition was an ROV named SuBastain.

SuBastain could dive 4,500 metres, far deeper than any human could go. Equipped with cameras and sensors, the robot explored the seafloor. The goal was to uncover new species and gather data to protect these fragile ecosystems.

The robot helped scientists document more than 100 species that had never been seen before. These included deep-sea corals, glass sponges, sea urchins, amphipods and squat lobsters.

Mind-blowing discoveries

The data collected by SuBastain is crucial for advancing Chile's marine protection efforts. The robot's ability to navigate the deep sea and collect samples has opened up new possibilities for marine science.

Each seamount that the robot explored hosted distinct ecosystems, many of which are vulnerable. By mapping 52,777 square kilometres of seafloor, the expedition resulted in the discovery of four new seamounts within Chilean waters. One seamount, named Solito, stood an impressive 3,530 metres tall.

The team was led by Dr Javier Sellanes from Chile's Universidad Católica del Norte (Catholic University of the North).

'We far exceeded our hopes on this expedition. You always expect to find new species in these remote and poorly explored areas, but the amount we found, especially for some groups such as sponges, is mind-blowing,' Javier says.

SuBastain's expeditions have revealed many species, including urchins (top: image courtesy Alex Ingle/Schmidt Ocean Institute) and a Chaunacops, a bony fish in the sea toad family (bottom: image courtesy Schmidt Ocean Institute)

Ethical questions: Staying safe and sound

The use of robotics in deep-sea exploration highlights their potential to revolutionise our understanding of the natural world. But as we continue to push the boundaries of exploration, we must consider the ethical implications of these powerful tools.

When we talk about robots, it's important to make sure they are safe, so that they can help us without causing any trouble. Just like we need to be careful when crossing the street, we need to make sure our robotic friends are safe so they don't accidentally hurt anyone. And just like we try to protect our computers from viruses, we need to protect robots from hackers who might try to make them do bad things.

What could we do if a robot started doing something it shouldn't? Should any human be able to shut any robot down at any time?

Robots in the air: The sky flyers

Airborne robots, also known as drones, take to the skies. Some fly low, hugging the ground, while others climb high into the atmosphere. Each of them gives us a different view of the land below.

How they move: Drones have spinning blades (like little helicopters) or wings (like aeroplanes) to zip through the air.

Finding their way: There are no roads in the air. Like the Maps app on a phone, these airborne robots use GPS. Sensors help keep them steady and flying straight at the right height – and make sure they don't bump into buildings!

How they see the world: Cameras take pictures and videos. Some drones can even 'see' heat or use a laser to measure distances. This technology is called LiDAR, which stands for **li**ght **d**etection **a**nd **r**anging.

Challenges: Drones have to battle strong winds. They must be light enough to stay up, but strong enough to not get tossed around. They also have to watch out for those other inhabitants of the sky – birds!

Unique considerations: Airborne robots must follow rules about where they can fly, and how to keep people safe. They need to communicate with GPS to know where they are, and they have to manage their battery life to stay in the air. Weather conditions such as wind and rain can affect their flying. The type of items they carry, like cameras or packages, also matters. Lastly, keeping data safe and making sure people feel comfortable with drones are important for everyone involved!

Drone robot in the air.

Ethical questions: Where does the buck stop?

When we send robots out to explore tough terrains, such as mountains or caves, they can thoroughly explore places that would be difficult or dangerous for us to access. But sometimes, accidents happen. Imagine if a robot caused a landslide or rockfall while exploring! This could destroy homes or even harm people caught in the way.

This raises important questions about accountability. If a robot accidentally causes damage in a sensitive area, who is responsible? Should it be the creators of the robot, or those who directed its exploration, even if the robot was itself autonomous?

SnotBot helps to save the whales

Ahoy! Thar she blows!

As the whale spouts through its blowhole, it sends up a plume of air, water vapour and snot. Just like snorting out of a giant nostril, blowing out helps the whale clear any biological material and allows it to take in fresh air. And when this happens, SnotBot the drone is waiting.

SnotBot flies through the plumes that whales exhale, collecting the snotty mess on small, flat petri dishes. Back at the lab, scientists will study the whale boogers that SnotBot brought back. Amazingly, this little pile of goo can reveal a whole lot about the whale, including whether it is sick or healthy.

For starters, the researchers can study the whale's DNA. DNA is like a set of instructions inside every living thing that makes them who they are. Whale snot also contains hormones, which are biological chemicals that give information such as whether the whale is stressed, or if a female whale might be expecting a baby!

The snot provides a glimpse into the whale's microbiome. A microbiome is made up of all the different microorganisms, including bacteria, that live inside an animal.

SnotBot is super helpful for whale scientists, because they can learn a lot without having to annoy them or even touch them! Because whales (and dolphins) are facing growing threats, from pollution to getting tangled in fishing nets, tools such as this drone can make a big difference.

Andy Rogan is the principal scientist for the SnotBot program. In 2017, he shot a documentary with National Geographic called *Earth Live*.

Andy remembers that when the show aired, a viewer tweeted 'SnotBot is what makes kids want to become scientists'.

'I think this quote typifies what I am most proud of with SnotBot,' he says. 'It has engaged and inspired so many people – and instilled in them a sense of awe and curiosity about the natural world.'

When the whale exhales, SnotBot collects snot to study in the lab. (Image courtesy Ocean Alliance)

Battling bushfires with robots

Imagine a blistering summer day in the heart of Australia. The air is thick with heat. Temperatures soar to 45 degrees Celsius. The wind howls at speeds up to 80 kilometres per hour, whipping through the dry, brittle vegetation. The landscape, already parched and crackling underfoot, becomes a tinderbox – ready to ignite.

When a bushfire starts, it consumes everything in its path. It spreads quickly, driven by the relentless wind, the abundance of dry fuel and the rugged terrain. Firefighters work hard to control these fires, but it's a dangerous job. They need to know exactly where the fire is, how fast it's moving and in which direction, and how much fuel (wood and other flammable materials) is in its path. But getting this information isn't always easy or safe.

Now imagine a firefighting robot that could gather crucial information before and during bushfires, all while keeping humans out of harm's way. That's exactly what the international team of researchers in the SILVANUS Project is working on.

Robots on the move

As part of the project, scientists from CSIRO's Data61 are designing robots that can move into fire zones. The robots come in different shapes and sizes – some walk on legs, others move on tracks, and drones fly above. Once they reach the fire, they send back as much information as possible to the firefighters. Dr Paulo Borges from CSIRO explains that a big challenge the team faced was preparing the robots to confront soaring temperatures and rough landscapes.

The robots have to be smart, move independently, navigate tricky terrain and avoid obstacles. They also had to be equipped with sensors to ensure they sent back useful information. They use LiDAR, cameras and other sensors to capture images, find their exact location, and measure tree and leaf density (how dense, or thick, the bush is).

'To be able to localise and navigate, we have to combine LiDARs with something called IMU, which stands for **i**nertial **m**easurement **u**nit,' Paulo explains.

Robots could be used to scout areas ahead of bushfires where firefighters cannot safely go. (Image courtesy CSIRO)

IMU measures rotations and accelerations. It helps the robots navigate well by combining information about the world (from the sensors) with information on its own 'body' or frame, through the IMU.

Firefighting robots have to be fast and easy to deploy.

'If you're operating in firefighting, it's not something that you can take your time and have a cup of coffee while you wait,' says Paulo. 'It is intense, and you have to respond fast. So, our robots had to be user-friendly and easy to use. You should be able to just set them up and send them out to do their job.'

A bird's eye view

All the information collected by the robot is sent back to a cloud-based platform that firefighters can monitor from a safe distance.

Tom Lowe, a senior experimental scientist, explains that these robots can go into areas too dangerous for humans. 'Using this online platform, you can see a map of what the ground robots have found,' he says.

'If you had a number of these ground robots scouting in front of a fire, you'd have a tremendous amount of information at your fingertips. Then you could combine it with data from a drone overhead, and even crowd-sourced information from social media.'

'Twenty years ago, people wouldn't have expected aerial drones to be used in firefighting like they are now. And the drones are probably 10 years ahead of ground robots.'

Although these robots are still being developed, Tom believes they could be fighting real fires in the next few years.

The future of firefighting

Researchers from Europe, Australia, Indonesia and Brazil are coming together as part of the global SILVANUS Project. They aim to help authorities make better decisions and respond quickly when wildfires break out.

The project combines wireless communication, remote detection and fire behaviour modelling, and is named after 'Silvanus', the Roman god of woods and protector of the forest. The data collected from drones and ground robots is combined into a single online platform for fire authorities.

The team is also working with researchers in the Czech Republic to develop 'swarm robotics' technology. This means many robots can work together, like a swarm of insects, to cover large areas and provide valuable information to firefighters.

Paulo says that since global warming is a big concern, climate experts involved in SILVANUS estimate that it is likely that we will unfortunately see more forest fires.

'Every time there's a fire, there's so much loss: not only to humans, but mainly to wildlife and vegetation. Some forest trees have been there for hundreds of years,' Paulo says.

'I am proud to be involved in an activity that tries to reduce the impact of global warming on our forests.'

Meet Jackie Dujmovic: Taking beach conservation to new heights

What do you do if you spot a shark near a beach?

If there isn't a lifeguard around, you could run down the beach screaming at people in the water. Or you could jump up and down and wave your hands.

Jackie Dujmovic thinks we can do one better – we could use a UAV.

What's a UAV? It stands for **u**nmanned **a**erial **v**ehicle, and is a type of drone. Jackie fell in love with them when she bought her first UAV back in 2015.

'I made a split-second decision that this is what I was going to do,' she recalls. 'The next day I went out to get my UAV licence and started setting up a business.'

Today, Jackie is the founder and head of her own company, Hover UAV, which is a leading global company in drone operations. Based in Queensland, the company explores the possibilities of drones and robotics.

Danger in the water!

Jackie loves to work with drones because they help her solve challenges and save lives. Take the shark attack scenario we mentioned; Jackie actually did something about it.

'I designed and commissioned a shark alarm that could be installed on any UAV platform,' Jackie explained. 'I'm not an electronics expert, but I had the idea and I knew how it could work with drones.'

In 2018, this innovation earned Jackie a spot on the global Women to Watch in UAS List. (UAS stands for **u**nmanned **a**erial **s**ystems.)

Her team has since used drones to study marine conservation, looking at shark migrations, whale movements and marine debris. They have also worked out what type of marine animals live along the New South Wales coastline in Australia.

Jackie set up and runs her own company, Hover UAV. (Image courtesy Jackie Dujmovic)

Drones for everyone

In the early years of Hover UAV, Jackie worked with many talented entrepreneurs and scientists.

'I love problem-solving, and I realised that many of their challenges were about getting their products to market,' she explains.

This inspired a shift in Jackie's thinking. She still loves flying drones, but she's also making drones accessible to everyone.

'My goal has become working with universities and companies. I want to break down the barriers and regulatory pathways so that drones can be used as everyday tools.'

Jackie admits that this has proven to be challenging. Many things must be considered when getting drones up in the air, especially for regular or large-scale use.

'How do we put them to work? How do we save money? How do we fly beyond the visual line of sight, and how does one pilot handle multiple drones? How do we add AI to automate them further?'

Ethical questions: Flying too high?

Drones are becoming increasingly important in emergency situations, where quick action can save lives. They can fly over rugged terrain to deliver medicine to remote areas that vehicles can't easily reach. This makes drones valuable tools during a crisis, but leaves important issues to consider.

When drones fly above backyards and farms, how do they respect people's privacy? Could drones pose a risk to wildlife? What happens if they crash or drop their cargo?

Find where you fit in the world

Jackie's team works with different businesses, from mining and electricity companies to government and agriculture, to help them reduce their workload and risk.

'A lot of these people have to go to risky sites. Using drones adds a level of safety and efficiency,' she explains.

Jackie has learned to trust her instincts. She says one key to her success has been her openness to try new things.

'I don't usually take "no" as an answer. I like taking chances, doing new things and pushing boundaries. You've got to find where you fit in the world.'

Jackie Dujmovic designed a shark alarm that could be installed on any UAV platform. (Image courtesy Jackie Dujmovic)

Space robots: Cosmic adventurers

Look up at the sky. Out there somewhere, a robot may be looking back at you. Ever since humans began exploring space, we have relied on robots to do some of the legwork.

From roving the Martian surface to orbiting distant planets, robots in space must withstand extreme conditions, such as intense radiation, and very high or low temperatures. They navigate using the stars and relay information back to Earth. The information takes a long time to get here, but it eventually reaches the robot researchers back here on Earth.

How they move: Curiosity, the Mars rover, has wheels to trundle over alien rocks and dust. The Voyager spacecraft doesn't land, but flies through space instead. It uses rockets to change direction, and solar panels to get energy from the Sun.

Finding their way: There's no GPS in space. So space robots navigate using a combination of star maps (just as ancient sailors did) and radio signals from Earth. They also use what is known as inertial navigation to track their movement and calculate their position based on their last location. Onboard sensors measure things such as distance to nearby objects, providing extra information to aid in navigation.

How they see the world: Their cameras can see different types of light (even types we can't see with our eyes). Their arms collect samples of alien soil, and their antennas send huge amounts of data back to Earth.

Challenges they face: Space is a tough place! No air, extremes of cold or heat, and lots of radiation. Robots in space need shields to protect them from the Sun's radiation, and are built with materials that can withstand massive changes in temperature. And of course no power plugs can be found up there – so our robots need batteries to run!

Unique considerations: Communicating with space robots can take a long time. When we send a message to a robot on Mars, it only takes 20 minutes to get there. But messaging a robot further out in the solar system could take up to four hours! Designers have to make sure these robots can make some decisions on their own while they wait for instructions from humans on Earth.

Space bots explore new frontiers

In 1957, the former Soviet Union (now known as Russia) sent the first robot into space. It was called Sputnik 1. A big metal ball, Sputnik 1 orbited Earth and made beeping sounds.

That beeping was the sound that kicked off the space age.

After the Apollo missions to the Moon ended in 1972, space robots really took over. These include rovers, which drive around on other planets; landers, which touch down and stay in one place; and orbiters, which fly around planets or moons. The robots run experiments, take selfies and even grab samples of rocks or dust to send back to Earth.

One big reason we send robots into space, rather than people, is that it's a lot safer. Space can be dangerous, and robots can withstand harsh conditions, such as extreme temperatures or high levels of radiation. They also don't need to breathe, or eat, like we do. And another big advantage? It's cheaper. Building a spaceship for people is expensive, but robots are cheaper because they are easier to send up – and we don't have to bring them back.

Perhaps you've heard about NASA's Mars rovers, including Perseverance and Curiosity. But these celebrated robots represent only a fraction of NASA's work. Behind the scenes, NASA engineers are tirelessly working on new robots.

Let's meet some of them.

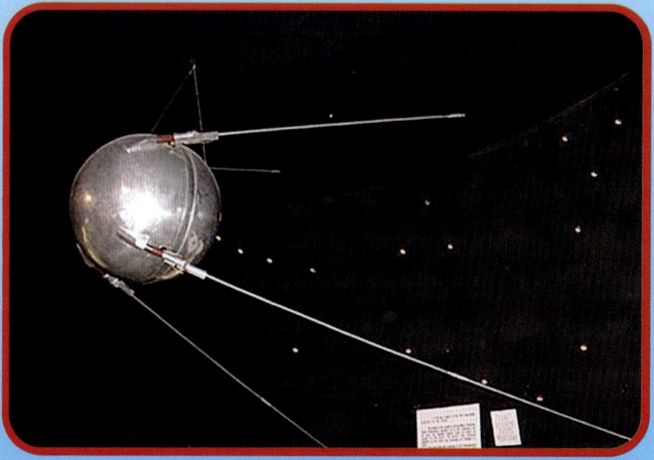

A replica of Sputnik 1 in the Museum of Cosmonautics and Rocket Technology, Saint Petersburg, Russia. (Photo by Andrew Butko via Wikimedia Commons, CC BY-SA 3.0)

NASA's Perseverance Mars rover took this selfie on 23 July 2024, the 1,218th Martian day, or sol, of the mission. (Image courtesy NASA/JPL-Caltech/MSSS)

This photo of NASA Mars Science Laboratory rover, Curiosity, was taken during testing on 3 June 2011. The turret at the end of Curiosity's robotic arm holds five devices. (Image courtesy NASA/JPL-Caltech)

Going where others fear to roll

It's stupendously expensive to send anything into space, so it makes sense to keep everything lightweight – and the smaller the better. The roboticists at NASA's JPL in California have figured out how to pack a robot into the tiniest space. Their strategy? Fold it up like a piece of origami paper!

Say hello to A-PUFFER, or the **a**utonomous **p**op-**u**p **f**lat **f**olding **e**xplorer **r**obot. The original robot – known as PUFFER – had four wheels, but A-PUFFER has two. This allows it to climb steep slopes. And if it's time to crawl? The wheels can be folded over the main body. A-PUFFER even has a tail for stability. And the whole robot, tail and all, is small enough to fit into a shoebox!

Each A-PUFFER robot has an onboard computer, a wireless radio for communication and a camera for sensing the environment. It packs down nearly flat for transport, and then re-expands on-site. These mini-robots would be ideal companions for larger rovers. Once they're on a new planet or moon, the A-PUFFER will be ready to crawl up sand dunes or explore a steep crater – anywhere a larger rover simply can't fit.

Researchers are teaching PUFFERs how to work together in a swarm, just like bees. Something like a steep cliff face might defeat an individual robot. However, if PUFFERs could link up like rock climbers and work together, they could climb that wall.

Ethical questions: Goodbye robot

Concern is growing about space debris and the environmental impact of sending robots and other devices into space.

What is our responsibility when it comes to maintaining space as a clean, safe environment – avoiding cluttering orbits with inactive satellites and old robots? Sometimes, we even send robots to places where we can't ever get them back – it's simply too expensive or too difficult to do so.

What ideas do you have for cleaning up old satellites and space robots that are no longer working? How can we prevent space from becoming a floating garbage heap?

A shoebox-sized, wheeled robot explores the rugged terrain on the surface of NASA's Mars Yard during recent tests of the A-PUFFER project. The robots are designed to work in groups, and could form roving teams of small robots that might one day explore the surface of the Moon or Mars. (Image courtesy NASA/JPL-Caltech)

Ready for a moon shot

Jean-Pierre de la Croix (see p. 35) was the project manager for A-PUFFER, and is now working on CADRE. CADRE stands for **c**ooperative **a**utonomous **d**istributed **r**obotic **e**xploration. It's quite a mouthful, but the word to focus on here is 'cooperative'. This isn't about just one robot – it's a team!

Jean-Pierre explains that CADRE is made up of a network of small rovers. Equipped with solar panels, they draw their energy from the Sun. They have four wheels, cameras, navigation sensors and a device known as a multistatic, ground-penetrating radar. This is a bit like an X-ray machine, but instead of identifying broken bones, it uses many little antennas to see what's hiding under the ground.

Together, these tools will help the rovers map the lunar terrain in 3D. And it's all packed into robots the size of a small suitcase!

The CADRE bots can communicate with each other and a lunar lander using radios. They're also mostly autonomous – they don't need constant directions from people to do their job.

And what is the job? To take measurements of different locations. By working as a team, they can collect more data and cover more ground than any single robot could. Jean-Pierre hopes this experiment could pave the way for autonomous, multi-robot missions. These missions could enter unexplored or risky terrain and support astronauts.

'I'm most excited about demonstrating that autonomous rovers can work as teams to allow us to gather science data in a way that wasn't possible before,' he says. 'And to inspire everyone to think about what new exploration and science they could achieve with a team of robots!'

CADRE rovers undergo tests in a cleanroom, to ensure there's no contamination from dust, germs or other particles.

Assembling a CADRE rover for upcoming trials.

Lifting a CADRE rover into place for testing.

Two CADRE rovers tackle Mars-like terrain.

Meet Lauren Hanson: An out-of-this-world journey

As a child, Lauren Hanson loved building things with LEGO, and taking apart things to see how they worked. As an adult, she finished university with not one degree, but two!

Lauren now has qualifications in Mechanical Engineering and Science from Monash University. As head of the Monash 'Nova Rover' team, she got a taste for robotics (and leadership).

More than half the members of the Monash Nova Rovers were studying engineering, but they needed other disciplines too – including science, accounting and medicine! Together, they went all-out to compete in robotics competitions.

After graduation, Lauren went on to work as a Design Engineer at Gilmour Space Technologies. There, she designed nifty stuff such as rocket engines and orbital launch vehicles. Today, she's leader of the Robotic Design Team at CSIRO, Australia's National Science Agency.

Wait ... what's an orbital launch vehicle?

An orbital launch vehicle is a very strong spaceship that's built to take satellites, cargo or people into space.
It can put them into orbit around the Moon, Earth or other planets. You can think of them as cosmic delivery trucks – they do the heavy lifting, so we can have everything we need for research in space right on hand.

Lauren has worked on some exciting robotics projects since 2020, including a mission to the International Space Station (ISS). She works on tools to support scientists conducting experiments in space.

'I really like the problem solving,' Lauren says. 'And because it's research, we're always doing something new and different. It's almost impossible to get bored!'

Brilliant minds don't always think alike

Lauren's team is made up of people with many different specialities. These include engineers who specialise in electrical engineering or mechanical engineering, or software development. The robots they design together are as different as the environments they design them for.

Right now, Lauren's team are designing robots that are meant to work in space. That brings its own challenges. For instance, the team know they have to avoid flammable materials on spacecraft. They must also plan for extreme swings in temperature, the absence of Earth's gravity and even how radiation in space affects the electrical components in machines.

Solving these difficult problems takes lots of time – and trial and error.

'If you're not failing, it can mean you're not learning,' Lauren says. 'Sometimes you learn more from failure than you do from success.'

She remembers being told to 'fail fast and fail often' – meaning you were picking up big issues early on in the process. It's what allowed her to solve problems and eventually succeed.

Lauren believes that diverse teams are essential. When we bring together people from a range of backgrounds and experiences, we are more likely to think outside the box – and come up with better solutions.

Lauren says her love of problem solving drew her to research – it's almost impossible to get bored! (Image courtesy Lauren Hanson)

Astrobee: The robotic helper aboard the ISS

Astrobee is a robotic free flyer. Unlike many other items on the International Space Station (ISS), it doesn't have to be tied down or controlled with wires. Instead, it has fans that propel it gracefully through the microgravity environment found on the ISS.

Robots on the ISS are designed to help astronauts and scientists carry out research, maintenance and other tasks. It can make life all that much easier for humans working in space stations.

Three Astrobees are aboard the station. Appropriately, their names are Honey, Queen and Bumble. Each cube-shaped robot has one arm that can grab and hold things, and allows them to anchor themselves to handrails to conserve energy. Cameras and sensors help them move around without bumping into things – or people. And they each have a docking station where they can recharge.

What roboticists learn from Astrobee's successes and failures will help develop the robot further!

Pushing the boundaries of technology in space

Robots such as Astrobee are critical to future space exploration. They'll be valuable members of the team when we return to the Moon or undertake deep space missions.

For example, let's look at the Lunar Gateway – a space station that will go around the Moon!

NASA plans to build this pit stop for astronauts – a place where they can live and work on the Moon, and maybe even explore deeper into space. Scientists will also use it to do cool experiments, engineers will develop new space gadgets and people from different countries will be able to work together. They already do this on the ISS, but this time, it's all about the Moon!

'When we're thinking about the Lunar Gateway, we know it's unlikely humans will be there all the time. And we don't want to be sending people off to the Moon, and just crossing our fingers and hoping the Lunar Gateway will be ready and waiting for them,' says Lauren Hanson.

'We want someone – or something – there to be monitoring it at all times and that everything is where it should be. So, we can trust that when we send humans, it's going to be safe for them.'

Lauren and her team are working on how we can map and monitor the interiors of such space stations and crafts from a distance. For her, it's a fascinating chance to push the boundaries of technology.

'We've done amazing things on Earth with robotics. Now we're proving that we can do them in space.'

A free-flying Astrobee robot pictured aboard the International Space Station. (Image courtesy NASA)

Robots in our bodies: Helping us stay healthy

Your body is an environment that's as unique – and challenging – as any of the others we have talked about so far. Medical robots are designed to work with and in our bodies. Robotic surgeons are a great example, and help doctors save lives in the operating theatre.

Then there's a new generation of minuscule machines known as microbots, which actually enter our body. They have the potential to revolutionise the way doctors diagnose and treat various health conditions.

Part of the challenge with these robots is the human element. Doctors and medical staff need extensive training to operate these systems effectively. This includes understanding the robots' abilities and limitations, as well as learning how to skilfully control them.

How they move: Bigger robots rely on human beings to help direct them. Smaller ones might be able flow along with the bloodstream. Others might be controlled externally using magnetic fields, allowing doctors to steer them to specific areas of the body.

How they find their way: Navigating the complex and twisting pathways of the human body is a challenge. Robots used in surgery are inserted through small incisions in the patient's skin, rather than large openings. This helps reduce recovery time, scarring and infection risks compared with traditional surgery.

How they see the world: Some medical robots use miniature cameras to see where they're going. Others are guided by external imaging techniques, such as MRI (magnetic resonance imaging) or ultrasound. These technologies let doctors track the robot's location from outside the body in real time. Sensors allow the robot to detect changes in temperature or chemistry. This is helpful for identifying different body tissues (such as skin and muscles), and monitoring vital signs (such as blood pressure, heart rate or body temperature).

Challenges they face: The human body is a complex environment, filled with blood, various fluids and delicate organs. Surgical robots used in operations must be exceptionally precise to avoid causing any harm. Nanobots, which operate at an even smaller scale, need to navigate through the bloodstream and reach specific areas without hurting the surrounding healthy cells or tissues. This requires advanced control mechanisms and the ability to precisely target a certain part of the body.

Unique considerations: Powering these robots depends on their size. As you can imagine, external ones are easier to power. Inside the body, nanorobots need to have tiny batteries, or get energy wirelessly from outside the body. And once they've done their job, they must be safely removed or dissolved in the body without causing any problems.

Microscopic marvels: The journey of microrobots in medicine

In the labs of University of Colorado Boulder, a team of skilled engineers has been working on something remarkable. They are creating tiny, self-propelled robots that can travel through liquids at impressive speeds.

Their goal? To potentially deliver medicines to those hard-to-reach places inside the human body.

Innovative engineering

These tiny health care assistants, also called microrobots, were recently described in a scientific publication called *Small*. Measuring only 20 micrometres wide, they are much thinner than a human hair. They are also incredibly fast. Travelling about 3 millimetres per second, they are the speedsters of the microscopic world.

So how do they move so fast? Made using a method that's like 3D printing, they are shaped like tiny rockets with three fins, and carry a small bubble of trapped air. The researchers expose the microrobots to an acoustic field, which is the area around any object that is making a sound. In response, the bubble of trapped air vibrates. This propels the robots forward at high speeds.

The researchers have already used the robots to transport medicine inside the bladders of lab mice. One day soon they might be treating diseases inside the human body!

A focus on health

The researchers also looked at bladder diseases, which are a common human health issue. Your bladder is like a bag that stores wee until you need to pee.

In their experiments, they sent thousands of microrobots into the bladders of laboratory mice. Each microrobot contained a tiny amount of a medicine called dexamethasone. The robots stuck to the bladder walls and slowly released the medicine over two days. This method could mean human patients could be treated more effectively, because they wouldn't have to visit their doctor as often.

The team is working on making these microrobots fully biodegradable. This means that after performing their task, they can safely dissolve in the body, leaving no trace behind.

With this type of research we're totally reimagining the future of medicine. Who knows what's in store?

Innovation amid crisis: Julie Dalsgard and the rise of Lifeline Robotics

In the spring of 2020, Denmark, like much of the world, found itself grappling with the rapid spread of COVID-19. Despite having a strong public health care system, the country faced a challenge they had never seen before as the number of infected people surged.

'We usually take pride in having a public health care system of a very high standard,' recalls Julie Dalsgard, who was completing her engineering degree at the time.

'Initially, most Danes [people from Denmark] thought the pandemic would not be that big of an issue for our hospitals. But week after week, the pandemic came closer, and dreadful images from Italy made their way to the Danish mass media.'

Testing troubles

As testing became a crucial part of managing the outbreak, the demand for manual labour skyrocketed.

'Testing was free of charge and the entire flow was digitised and fairly fast,' Julie says. However, the need for human hands to collect the samples created significant delays.

'Health care professionals were already overrun at the hospitals, so young people were recruited,' she explains.

'This sudden demand showed me the critical challenge of delivering a simple health care service to an entire population within a fixed time.'

A lightbulb moment

These challenges got Julie thinking: Could robotics help reduce the strain on health care systems during such a crisis? She says that the lack of people able to work, and the repetitive nature of many hospital tasks, are important considerations when thinking about the use of robotics.

Julie wasn't the first person to have this thought. It led her to a company called Lifeline Robotics, which was hard at work in the field. She joined them once she finished university, and is now head of the company.

'I had no previous experience before working at Lifeline Robotics. The first few months I worked on different tasks, but after four months, the former CEO asked me if I wanted to take over after him,' she recalls.

Despite feeling unprepared, Julie took on the challenge. She broke tasks into manageable sizes and learned to navigate the responsibilities step by step.

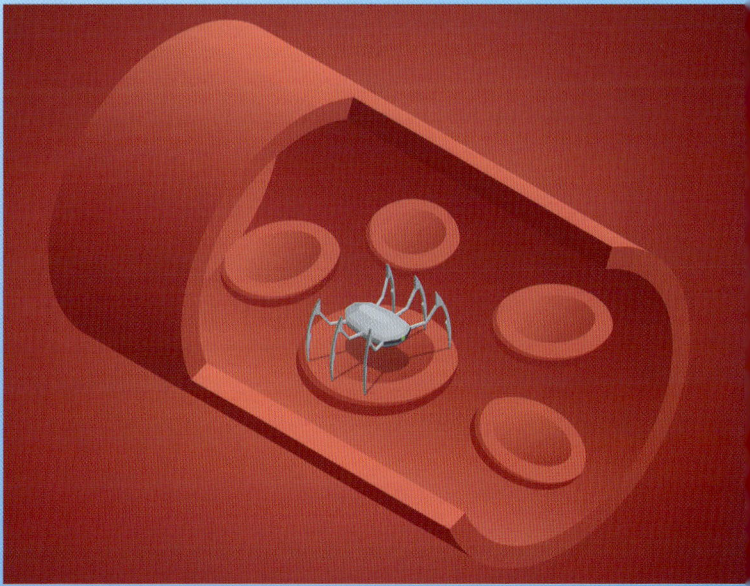

A microrobot inside a blood vessel.

Robots on the frontlines of COVID-19

In the early months of 2020, COVID-19 started spreading rapidly. It didn't just affect people's health, it changed how hospitals operated. In some cases, this meant calling in the robots!

Why? Well, robots have some great advantages. The main one is that they don't catch viruses like people do. They don't fall ill, and are super easy to clean.

Robots helped people in many ways during the COVID-19 pandemic. Some monitored patients in hospitals, while others disinfected hospital rooms. This was a big help to medical workers, reducing their risk of getting the virus.

A helping hand

Let's zoom into Kigali, a town in Rwanda, Africa. A squad of robots became the first line of defence against the virus at a medical centre. Made by UBTECH Robotics in China, these robots could check someone's temperature, deliver food and medication to patients, capture video and audio and notify hospital staff when they thought a patient needed attention.

In Denmark, a team of doctors and engineers created a throat-swab robot to speed up COVID-19 testing. A swab (pronounced swob) is a small piece of soft material on a stick, such as the cotton buds used to clean the outsides of your ears. Using advanced tech such as computer vision and machine learning, the robot can find the perfect spot in the throat for a swab. Then, it collects the sample with a robotic arm. The method is quicker and more consistent than human testing. Made by a company appropriately called Lifeline Robotics, SwabBot is also quick and easy to clean and disinfect.

In Italy, a hospital in Sardinia received some high-tech help from robots during the pandemic. Developed by UVD Robots, they had their own navigation system and powerful ultraviolet-C lights. This light can kill viruses and other harmful organisms by destroying their genetic material. With these robots, intensive care units and operating theatres in hospitals could be cleaner and safer.

Robots also took over repetitive tasks in hospitals, such as in Shenzhen, China, and near Austin, Texas. For example, in Texas, the Moxi robot, made by Diligent Robotics, tirelessly delivered supplies to patient rooms. This allowed staff to focus on patient care.

In northern Italy, a region severely affected by the COVID-19 crisis, doctors and nurses employed robots as their stand-ins to monitor patients. These robots, made by the Chinese firm Sanbot, had cameras and microphones and could even access patient data. This was a great way to minimise exposure to the virus and save on protective equipment.

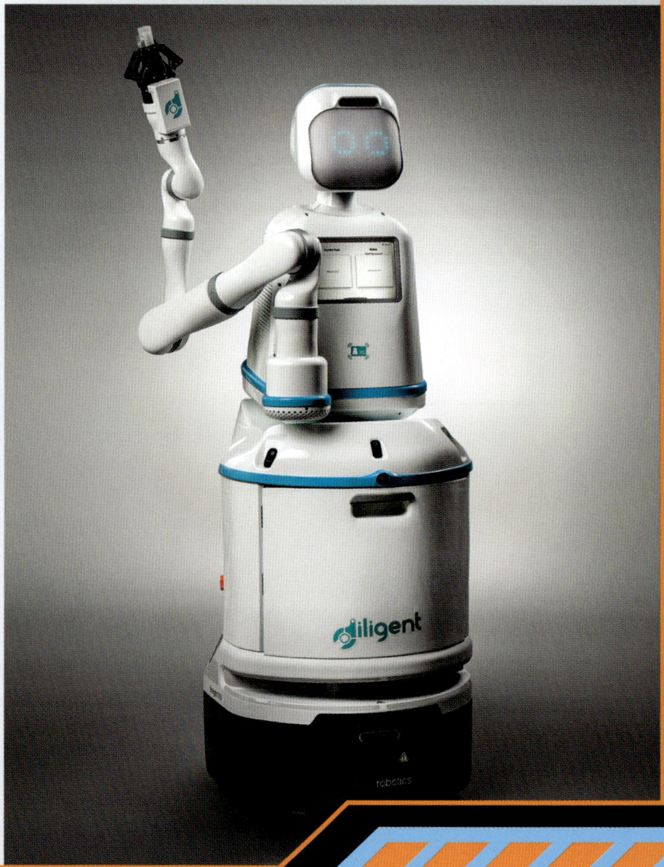

Moxi is a mobile robot designed to take on some of the frequent and repetitive tasks that nurses must perform. (Image courtesy Diligent Robotics)

Meet SwabBot!

The development of the company's throat-swab robot was gentler than manual testing, where a human sticks the swab in your throat.

'Having a throat-swab sample is never going to be a pleasant experience, but most people say the robotic procedure is more comfortable than the manual sample,' Julie notes.

The robot's ability to deliver the same procedure every time with just the right amount of pressure means samples are of a high quality and more consistent.

Julie agrees that using robots in medicine has ethical challenges.

'Creating a robotics solution for medicine is about providing better opportunities for receiving health care without the need for a doctor or nurse. We use vision and AI in our solution, ensuring it does not discriminate against any individual,' she explains.

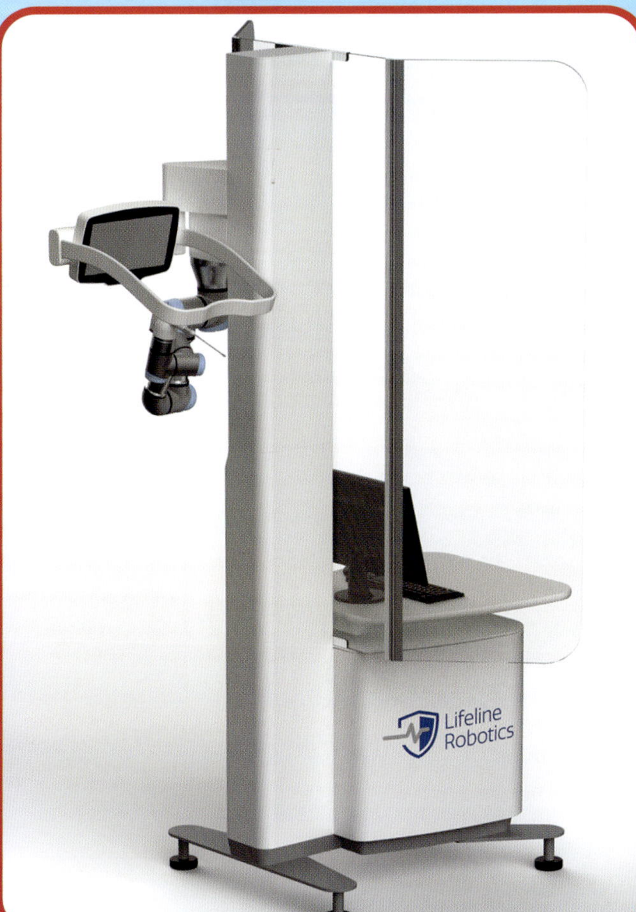

Ethical questions: Fair play

Just like us, robots learn from what they see and hear. But what if they learn something that's not fair, or treat some people better than others? We need to teach robots to treat everyone equally. It is important to train them correctly. AI systems and robots can accidentally pick up biases, just like humans. Bias occurs when you form an opinion about whether a person, group or idea is good or bad, and treat them in different ways. This happens when the people who make robots use a lot of information or data that isn't diverse enough.

Think about it like this: if you only ever read books about the ocean, you might not know much about the mountains or the desert, right? It's the same with robots. If a medical AI learns to diagnose skin conditions using only pictures of lighter skin, it might miss or misinterpret the same conditions on darker skin – leading to mistakes in diagnosis and treatment.

This tells us something really important. When scientists and engineers make robots, they need to use a wide mix of information from all sorts of people and places. That way, the robots will be smarter and fairer.

Why do you think it's important for hospital and medical robots to know about all kinds of people? How can we help these robots learn about everyone to make sure they treat everyone the same way?

SwabBot's approach is quicker and more consistent than human testing. (Image courtesy Lifeline Robotics)

09 The future from here

We're nearly at the end of our journey through the world of robotics. Through the pages of this book, we've travelled from the dusty floors of ancient workshops to the vast expanse of outer space, uncovering the marvels of robotics at every turn. Let's take a moment to reflect on everything we've learned – and imagine what might lie ahead.

What we've discovered

We've seen how robots can take on dangerous jobs, making our world a safer and cleaner place. We've marvelled at their ability to dive deep into the oceans, soar through the skies and even venture into the human body, including places where it's too risky or impossible for humans to go.

Now you know how robots 'think', 'feel' and 'learn' – and how they do it differently from you. While they may not have brains or emotions like us, they can still process information and adapt to new challenges.

We looked at how robots navigate different environments. Roboticists designed them with specific challenges in mind, so that whether the robots were exploring space, under water or travelling underground, each had its own characteristics.

The use of robots is only as limited as our imagination. People are going to keep finding new and creative ways to work with these machines.

Diverse minds shaping the future

The story of robotics isn't just a story of machines – it's a story of people. We've also learned about the ingenious people behind these creations – the roboticists. Blending science, engineering and creativity, they are solving some of the world's most complex problems and inventing new ways of seeing the world.

Some roboticists have drawn on nature to inspire their designs, learning from bees, fish, birds and even human bodies to build robots that can accomplish complicated tasks.

Each roboticist's life experience fuels their problem-solving abilities, leading to creative breakthroughs. We discovered roboticists are drawn from many different disciplines: engineering, biology, ethics, coding, design and more. Working together helps to advance the field of robotics.

Ethical questions and opportunities

Along the way, we've also encountered important ethical questions. How do we ensure privacy in a world where robots can see and hear? What jobs will humans do if robots can perform tasks more efficiently than us? How do we make sure robots are used for good, helping rather than harming?

These questions don't have easy answers, but they remind us of the responsibility that comes with innovation. As we look to the future, it's up to all of us – scientists, engineers, policymakers and citizens – to guide the development of robotics in ways that benefit everyone.

The future of robotics

What does the future hold? Will we see robots that are even more intelligent and versatile? Even as you read this, we're finding new ways for humans and robots to work together, enhancing our abilities and opening up new frontiers.

As we close this book, I hope you're inspired by the incredible journey of robotics. From the pages of ancient myths to the laboratories of today, robots have captured our imagination and pushed the boundaries of what's possible.

Remember, the story of robotics is still being written, and you could be a part of it. Whether you dream of designing robots, solving ethical dilemmas or simply exploring the world with a curious mind, the future is yours to shape.

Thank you for joining me on this adventure! Let's keep dreaming, learning and creating together – who knows what we might discover next?

Glossary

Actuator: A device that moves or controls a mechanism or system

Algorithm: A set of rules or steps used to solve a problem or perform a task

Artificial intelligence: The ability of machines to perform tasks that normally require human intelligence

Autonomous: Able to perform tasks without human control

Battery: A device that stores and provides electrical energy

Biofabrication: Manufacturing biological products

Biomimicry: Designing products inspired by nature's systems and processes

Bionic: Combining biological and electronic parts to improve human functions

Circuit: A path that allows electricity to flow through connected components

Cleanroom: A special room where the air is kept very clean to stop dust, germs and other tiny particles from getting in

Code: Instructions written in a programming language for computers to follow

Computing: Using computers to process data and perform calculations

Crustacean: A group of aquatic animals with hard shells, such as crabs and lobsters

Drone: An unmanned aircraft that can be controlled remotely or fly autonomously

Engineer: A person who designs, builds or maintains engines, machines or structures

Ethics: The study of what is morally right and wrong. An ethicist is a person who specialises in studying ethics

Fire behaviour modelling: Using a computer model to simulate how fire spreads and behaves to improve safety and response

GPS: A system that uses satellites to determine exact locations on Earth

Hexapod: A robot with six legs designed for stability and adaptability

Hydraulics: A way of using liquids, usually oil or water, to create movement or power machines

Innovate: To introduce new ideas, methods or products

Interstellar: Related to or located between stars

LiDAR: Technology using laser light to measure distances and create detailed maps

Lunar Gateway: A planned space station orbiting the Moon to support lunar exploration

Machine: A device with moving parts that performs a task

Machine learning: The process of teaching computers to learn from data, and make predictions or decisions without being programmed to follow exact instructions

Mechanical: Related to machines or the principles of mechanics

Meltdown: A severe overheating of a nuclear reactor core, causing it to melt

Microrobot: A very small robot designed to perform precise tasks

MRI: A medical imaging technique that uses magnetic fields to 'see' internal structures

Natural language processing: The field of computer science that deals with the interaction between computers and human (natural) languages

Neuroscience: The study of the nervous system, including the brain

Nuclear: Related to the energy released during nuclear reactions

Nuclear power plant: A facility that generates electricity using nuclear energy

On-demand manufacturing: Producing goods as they are needed, rather than in advance

Orbit: The path an object takes as it revolves around another object in space

Poaching: Illegal hunting or capturing of wild animals

Privacy: The right to keep personal information confidential and protected

Programming: Writing instructions for a computer to carry out tasks

Prototype: An early model of a product used to test and refine ideas

Prototyping: Creating a prototype for testing and development

Quadruped: A robot with four legs designed for stability and mobility

Radiation: Energy emitted in the form of waves or particles

Radioactive material: Substances that release radiation as they decay

Remote detection: Identifying objects or conditions from a distance using technology

Roboethics: The ethics of how robots are designed, used and integrated into society

Robot: A machine able to carry out complex tasks automatically

Roboticist: A scientist or engineer who designs, builds and tests robots

Rocket: A vehicle propelled by the ejection of gases

Rover: A vehicle designed to explore the surface of a planet or moon

Sensing: Detecting and measuring changes in the environment

Sensor: A device that detects changes in its surroundings and sends information about those changes to another system or device

Simulation: The imitation of a real-world process or system for testing or training

Silicone: A synthetic material that is flexible and resists heat

Software architecture: The structure and design of software systems

Sonar: A technology that uses sound waves to detect objects underwater

Speech recognition: The ability of computers to understand spoken language

Technology: The application of scientific knowledge for practical purposes

Tracked vehicle: A vehicle that uses continuous tracks for movement

Tsunami: A large ocean wave caused by underwater earthquakes or volcanic activity

Ultrasound: Sound waves used in medical imaging

Wireless: Using radio waves to transmit data without wires

About the author

Here is something you should know about Smriti: she isn't a roboticist, but she had a lot of fun interviewing them for this book. It helps that she's been a journalist and writer for more than 15 years and isn't shy about asking silly questions. Smriti's byline has appeared in newspapers all over the world. She's been a Falling Walls Science Journalism Fellow (Germany), a Gabriel Garcia Márquez Cultural Journalism Fellow (Colombia) and a two-time winner of the Feature Writer of the Year Award.

Her name means memory in Sanskrit, and it's pronounced SMRITH-ee. She was born in India, lived in Sri Lanka and moved to Australia a few years ago. Based in Adelaide, she was lucky enough to work at the ABC and at CSIRO, Australia's national science agency.

This is her second book for younger readers (her first was about a boy living alongside Sri Lanka's wild elephants). She really hopes you'll enjoy reading this book as much as she enjoyed writing it.

Illustration credits

Circuit image, p. 3 and throughout: Jomic/Shutterstock.com

Drone, pp. 3 and 67: johavel/Shutterstock.com

SPOT robot dog, pp. 3 and 45: backwoods_design/Shutterstock.com

Humanoid robot, pp. 3 and 21: elenabsl/Shutterstock.com

Underwater robot, pp. 3 and 57: Macrovector/Shutterstock.com

Robotic arm, p. 3: graphixmania/Shutterstock.com

Robot with pencil, p. 5: RadovaniTalentino/Shutterstock.com

Open book, p. 6: ex_artist/Shutterstock.com

Robot, p. 6 and throughout: HappyPictures/Shutterstock.com

Inner workings of robot, p. 8: Cathy Larsen Design

Talos, p. 8: Cathy Larsen Design

Elephant clock (exterior and inner workings), p. 10: Cathy Larsen Design based on reference photos from richardreddingsantiques.com

Greek automatic maid, p. 11: Cathy Larsen Design based on reference photos from Kotsanas Museum of Ancient Greek Technology

The Writer (inner workings), p. 12: Cathy Larsen Design based on reference photos from Museum of Art and History of Neuchâtel

Robot, p. 15: HappyPictures/Shutterstock.com

Hexabot, p. 21: Cathy Larsen Design

Wheeled robot, pp. 21–23: Cathy Larsen Design

Microbot, p. 22: Cathy Larsen Design based on an image at https://www.robeaute.com/

Robotic arms on assembly line, p. 26: WinWin artlab/Shutterstock.com

Children with a drone, p. 27: Cathy Larsen Design based on image from LightField Studios/Shutterstock

Group of search and rescue robots, p. 30: Cathy Larsen Design artist's impressions of Sakura II by FuRo, Chiba Institute of Technology, Scorpion and Mini Manbou robots by Toshiba

Human–robot comparison, p. 45: Cathy Larsen Design; light globe and circuit by graphicriver_icons_logo/Shutterstock; books by Keysi/Shutterstock.com; computer by Diki Prayogo/Shutterstock.com

Rat and iRat, p. 55: Cathy Larsen Design based on iRat image courtesy of Professor Janet Wiles, University of Queensland

Autonomy, p. 57: Cathy Larsen Design

Adaptability, p. 57: bsd studio and Macrovector, both Shutterstock.com

Sensors and communication, p. 57: Cathy Larsen Design; radar image adapted from Flaticon.com; star map by shooarts/Shutterstock.com

Energy efficiency, p. 57: Cathy Larsen Design; battery image Yevheniia BH/Shutterstock.com

Robot in rough territory, p. 58: Cathy Larsen Design inspired by Deep Robotics robot dog 'Lynx'

Robot underwater, p. 66: Cathy Larsen Design inspired by underwater drones

Drone, p. 67: johavel/Shutterstock.com

Firefighting robot, p. 70: Cathy Larsen Design inspired by firefighting robots by CSIRO, RORI (Rio Tinto) and Colossus

Microrobot inside a blood vessel, p. 81: Golden Sikorka/Shutterstock.com

Front cover: (clockwise, from top right) Robotic arm illustration (graphixmania/Shutterstock.com); Robot illustration (HappyPictures/Shutterstock.com); NASA's Perseverance rover (NASA/JPL-Caltech/MSSS); Humanoid robot (elenabsl/Shutterstock.com); Colossus (Manon.vermenouze, Wikimedia Commons, CC BY-SA 4.0); SuBastian (Schmidt Ocean Institute, CC BY-SA 4.0); CSIRO robotic dog (CSIRO); SnotBot (Ocean Alliance); Drone illustration (johavel/Shutterstock.com); Moxi (Diligent Robotics)

Back cover: (top, left to right) Amelia Luu at work with a robot (Amelia Luu); Robotic systems at the DARPA challenge (Erin McColl/CSIRO); Lauren Hanson problem solving at work (Lauren Hanson); (bottom) Hexabot illustration (Cathy Larsen Design)

Index